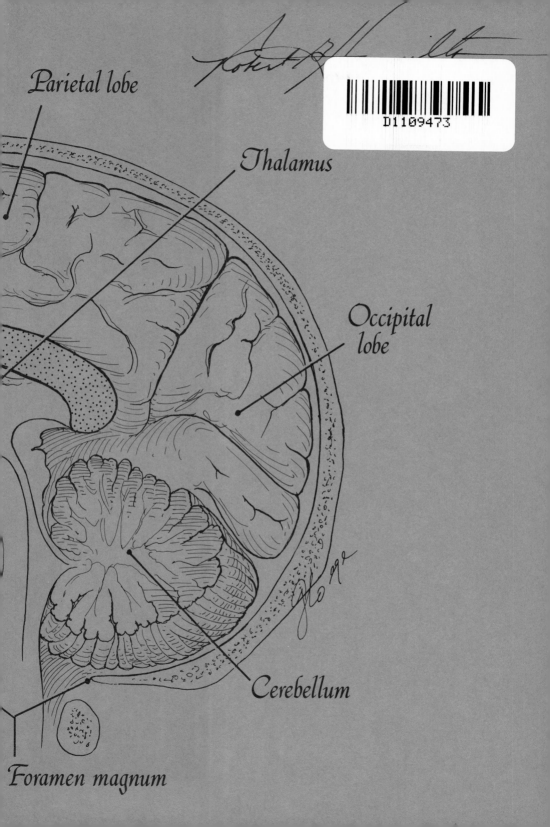

Parietal lobe

Thalamus

Occipital
lobe

Cerebellum

Foramen magnum

BRAIN MATTERS

BRAIN MATTERS

Stories of a Neurologist and His Patients

BRUCE H. DOBKIN, M.D.

CROWN PUBLISHERS, INC.
NEW YORK

Grateful acknowledgment is given for the following: The passage from "The Sisters," which appears on page 1, is an excerpt from *Dubliners* by James Joyce. Copyright 1916 by B. W. Huebsch. Definitive text copyright © 1967 by the Estate of James Joyce. Reprinted by permission of The Society of Authors as the literary representative of the Estate of James Joyce and Viking Penguin Inc. The poetry that appears on page 99 is an excerpt from *The Man of Many L's* by Maxine Kumin, which first appeared in *The Seattle Review,* vol. IV, no. 2, fall 1981. Copyright © 1981 by The Seattle Review.

Copyright © 1986 by Bruce H. Dobkin, M.D.

All rights reserved.
No part of this book may be reproduced
or transmitted in any form or
by any means, electronic or mechanical,
including photocopying, recording,
or by any information storage and retrieval system
without permission in writing from the publisher.

Published by Crown Publishers, Inc.,
225 Park Avenue South, New York, New York 10003
and represented in Canada by the Canadian MANDA Group

CROWN is a trademark of Crown Publishers, Inc.

Manufactured in the United States of America

Library of Congress Cataloging-in-Publication Data
Dobkin, Bruce H.
    Brain matters.

    1. Neurology—Popular works.   2. Neurology—Case
studies. I. Title. [DNLM: 1. Brain—popular works.
WL 300 D633b]
RC346.D63   1986   612'.82   86-11645
ISBN 0-517-55983-8

10 9 8 7 6 5 4 3 2 1

First Edition

Written so that Gladys, Craig, and Jane might understand more, dedicated to my wife for her remarkable support in all things, and to be read one day by Duke's grandchildren.

PART 1

Every night as I gazed up at the window I said softly to myself the word "paralysis." It had always sounded strangely in my ears, like the word "gnomon" in the Euclid and the word "simony" in the Catechism. But now it sounded to me like the name of some maleficent and sinful being. It filled me with fear, and yet I longed to be nearer to it and to look upon its deadly work.

JAMES JOYCE, *Dubliners*

ONE

I FINISHED OFF THE FIRST CANDY BAR I'd eaten in years. I crumpled the shiny red and white wrapper, held it over the passenger's seat with my eyes still on the road, and let it slide onto the floor. I'd bet that was how he did it.

In the summers after I turned into my teens, I had worked on one of my father's rug-cleaning trucks. Every evening as he drove us home, I'd gather five or six balled-up candy-bar wrappers from under my feet. He couldn't imagine, he'd say, how they had gotten there. We kept this secret between us, even when my mother asked why he was putting on so much weight.

The pager's atonal blasts startled me out of my commuter's reverie. I pulled out of traffic dominated by boat trailers and campers heading for a July weekend in the Southern California mountains and beaches. From a phone booth in a Chevron station, I dialed Laura May at my answering service.

"Hope I didn't get you at a bad time," she said, "but I've got a doctor on the line who insists on speaking to you."

"You know how much I enjoy your little love messages. Put him on."

"Dobkin? That you?" It was Jake Springstein, a crusty general practitioner, maybe the oldest on the Daniel Freeman Memorial Hospital staff. "I got this young fella who's been kinda weak the last two days."

Fifteen feet across the blacktop, a truck driver wearing an Angels baseball cap gunned his diesel engine. I jammed a finger in one ear, pressed the receiver tight against the other, and shouted, "Sorry, but I can barely hear you. I'm at a pay phone."

"I was saying," the G.P. continued in a deeper, hoarse voice, "when he first came by the office yesterday, he said he was weak. But he looked all right to me. His job wasn't going all that good, you know? Maybe it was just that, I figure." Springstein paused. I remembered how, when puzzled, Springstein would smooth his round face and bald scalp with his hands as if nurturing the skin with lotion after a shave. "Today he comes back and his muscle strength does seem down. Now, he had a bug a coupla weeks ago. But I don't think it's just that."

"What were his reflexes like?"

"He's got 'em. I'm calling you because he kinda struggled standing up from a chair this afternoon and he didn't do that yesterday. He looks fine otherwise. I've been taking care of Dick's family for thirty years. Maybe I'm getting too old to outwrestle my patients, but I can't break his muscle resistance except at the ankles. Anyway, I sent him home, but I'm thinking maybe we should admit him."

"Best thing to do," I agreed, unsure I'd gotten the whole story, between the traffic noise and Springstein's casual evaluation. A man was losing power; he might be on his way to total paralysis. The G.P. had second-guessed himself like doctors do almost daily with odd cases, and I respected his instincts. "Tell him I'll meet him in a half hour at the emergency room at Freeman. And to come prepared to stay overnight."

"Thanks. Name's Dick Gallagher. Only lives ten minutes away in Westchester. I'll come by after my dinner."

4

I called home and asked Barbara if she could push back our own meal to nine. She took this in stride, but added the slightly admonishing news that our year-old twins had just heard a car door slam and reacted by crawling to the back door, calling, "Dada."

The emergency room was quiet, a lull before Friday night created victims of payday celebrations. Dick Gallagher arrived minutes after me. Springstein's "young fella" was about my age, in his late thirties, but he walked like a hobbled calf, his hips swaying and his feet slapping against the linoleum floor. Gallagher's fashion-model-thin wife helped him climb onto the examining gurney and I drew the yellow curtains around us.

Three weeks ago, Gallagher said, he had run a low-grade temperature with runny nose and cough. Three days ago, he noticed a mild tingling in his toes and, by evening, in his fingers. The next morning at work, he stumbled getting out of his van and found it difficult to control a pencil or to handle a wire cutter or screwdriver. Dr. Springstein checked Gallagher's strength yesterday morning and said it seemed normal, except for some ankle weakness. But that night, he found himself unable to stand up from the soft sink of a deep living-room couch without a yank from his wife.

"The whole thing seems crazy." He smiled warily. "I was rock climbing out at Joshua Tree two weeks ago, doing some tough climbs, and now I can't get out of a chair."

"Which climbs did you make?" I asked.

"You know the area?"

"My brother and I've bouldered around there." This desert park near Palm Springs attracts aggressive climbers who take on steep, fifty- to one hundred-foot walls of coarse, tumescent granite christened with names like Urine Trouble, Jugular Vein, The Skull, and Brain Death. "You had to have been in good shape." He seemed relieved that I appreciated how much his strength had deteriorated. "Did you fall or injure your back or neck?"

"No. Missed a finger hold and dropped maybe six feet, but

my ropes caught me." Still at a loss for clues after asking other routine questions, I examined him.

I listened with my stethoscope for unusual sounds in his heart, lungs, belly, and blood vessels, palpated for lumps in his lymph nodes, belly, and over the nerves that cross his elbows and knees, and quickly inspected his skin and joints. Then I asked him to try and resist my tugging at his arms and legs. With a modest effort, I overcame my muscular patient's best efforts. When I broke the flagging resistance of his weakest muscles at the wrists and ankles with just two fingers, Sharon and Dick looked startled.

A neurologic exam—a head-to-toe tour of the anatomy and physiology of the nervous system hidden within the skull, spinal column, and muscles—would point me to the source of his weakness. Then I stood a better chance to figure out what caused it, because any one disease characteristically affects a particular part of the nervous system. So I began the exploratory journey at the surface of the two halves, or hemispheres, of his brain.

For centuries, the brain had been considered in various ages and cultures to be either a bag of marrow, the seat of good and bad humors, or the site of thought but not action. In 1870, two German researchers proved that a specific strip of the brain's outer layer, the motor cortex, was responsible for carrying out movements on opposite sides of the body. The toes and feet have their nerve cells in the trench between the tops of the hemispheres, and each body part sprawls out over the curvature of each half brain like an imprint of an upside-down baby with her thumb in her mouth. In humans, the nerve cells for speech and fine hand manipulations take up the most room. Patches of nerve cells, or neurons, in each frontal lobe's strip of motor cortex receive information from other neighboring patches of cells that interpret what we see, hear, feel, and remember. Any injury to this vast, interconnected system of around ten billion neurons, such as an infection, a toxin, a tumor, or an interruption in blood flow, can make the complex

6

physiology of the motor cortex falter. But in order to cause the weakness that Dick Gallagher complained of, the insult would also have entangled the so-called higher cortical functions— those bits and pieces of background information that direct our movements.

So I briefly screened Gallagher's intellect. Quickly and precisely, he repeated a phone number forward and backward. He recalled the word series "peaches, newspapers, and Chestnut Street" ten minutes after I directed him to remember it, followed a four-part instruction in the proper sequence, added ninety-eight plus nineteen correctly, named the parts of a wrist watch, generated a list of ten animals without hesitation, copied a drawing of superimposed circles, squares, and triangles, and interpreted the abstract meaning of several proverbs. Without evidence of some difficulty in his thinking, I was able to rule out the cortex as a possible location for Dick's weakness.

I climbed one rung down the neurological-exam ladder. Most smooth, well-learned movements—like standing up, hammering a nail, dancing, or climbing the steep face of a mountain—depend on at least three collections of neurons in each hemisphere: the cerebellum, the basal ganglia, and the thalamus.

From its nest in the back of the skull, tucked under the split loaf of the cerebral hemispheres, the cerebellum receives information about the tension in muscles, joints, and tendons and about any motion of the head, and passes it upward to the cortex. A diseased cerebellum causes drunklike loss of balance and clumsiness. If there's a problem in the almond-shaped basal ganglia, just beneath the cortex, people experience tremors and muscle rigidity, and they move slowly with a shuffling walk. The thalamus, the innermost group of cells deep within each hemisphere, receives information about everything we see, feel, and hear—whatever warrants our immediate attention—and acts like an intelligent switchboard that ties the cortex to almost every brain path involved in the coordination of movement.

To determine whether these deep centers of Gallagher's brain were involved, I tested his coordination. At my direction, he rapidly tapped each finger against the thumb of that hand, touched his index finger to mine as I changed its position in a game like pin-the-tail-on-the-donkey, precisely moved his finger back and forth from his nose to my stationary finger even with his eyes closed, sat still on the gurney without swaying, and walked a line steadily enough to pass a policeman's sobriety test. Gallagher's movements were slower than normal, but not clumsy. That eliminated the trio of cerebellum, basal ganglia, and thalamus from suspicion.

I moved another rung down the ladder to the brain stem, a three-inch-long root that connects the brain to the spinal cord. Every piece of information that travels to and from our limbs passes through the tens of millions of neuronal highways here. It is easiest to test the twelve cranial nerves that form within the brain stem and travel out through tiny perforations in the skull to move the muscles of the eyes, face, larynx, tongue, and palate, and bring in what our five senses appreciate. All but two of Gallagher's worked properly. When I asked him to puff out his cheeks, they collapsed too easily. And his voice had a hint of nasality, as if air seeped past a weakened palate near the back of his throat. Since the rest of the brain stem checked out okay, the site of damage was probably outside it, in just two of the peripheral cranial nerves.

At the next rung down, the spinal cord, I found no apparent signs of disease. But in the following step down, I closed in on the most likely location of Dick's problem. Gallagher could not tell the difference between a sharp and a blunt point poked against his hands and feet. And when I moved the joints of his toes and fingers up and down, he couldn't tell me which way I was moving them without looking. But higher up on his ankles and wrists he perceived these sensations normally; his sensory loss was confined to his hands and feet, as if he wore gloves and stockings that muffled feeling.

Microscopic receptors in the skin, joints, tendons, and muscles send raw data into the spinal cord about touch, texture, temperature, and pain along the sensory component of the so-called peripheral nervous system. These receptors constantly, automatically report to the cerebellum and thalamus the tension in the muscles and the position of the joints, so we don't tilt over or collapse under our own weight. While sensory information travels into the spinal cord along the glistening white peripheral-nerve highways, the final instructions for movement simultaneously travel out from neurons in the spinal cord along parallel peripheral-nerve lanes that connect to the muscles of the body. When the peripheral nerves are under attack by some disease, the longest ones, which reach to the fingers and toes, usually suffer first. So Gallagher's loss of sensation and strength, most severe in his hands and feet, pointed toward a problem in the peripheral nerves in his arms and legs. His reflexes confirmed this.

The deep tendon reflexes, at the bottom of the neurologic-exam ladder, are the purest, most primitive body movement. A gentle tap with a reflex hammer at the elbow, knee, or ankle stretches a muscle tendon. The sensory receptor in the tendon also changes shape and, like a depressed door-bell button, sends an electrical signal up the limb's peripheral-nerve wires. A ball of sensory neurons just outside the spinal cord receives this signal. These sensory neurons immediately transmit it to specific spinal-cord neurons, which automatically fire a brief volley of electrical impulses back out through the same peripheral nerve to the muscle of the tapped tendon. With this loop completed, the joint jerks involuntarily.

Gallagher had no tendon reflexes at his knees and ankles, and they just barely jerked at his elbows. My journey was complete; his disease had to be located within the broken loop of the primitive-reflex path, and was probably confined to the peripheral nerves themselves.

Leaning back, with palms flat against the gurney's mattress, Dick asked, "So what's the story? I'm pretty weak, aren't I?" Sharon put her hand on his thigh.

9

"It seems that the nerves that run out from the spinal cord to contract your muscles and that bring back information about what you feel in your skin and joints are being damaged. I suspect that when your body's immune system geared up to destroy the virus you had a few weeks ago, it probably produced substances that also inflamed your nerves. Remember the Swine Flu vaccine the government rushed into use when Ford was president?" He nodded. "It caused a flurry of cases of this, what we call the Guillain-Barré syndrome, because a protein in the inoculation aroused white cells in the blood circulation to react against peripheral nerves."

Sharon asked, "Will he get any weaker?"

I decided to explain not only his present state, but also the worst possible outcome. A rock climber knew how to deal with fear. "From what you have told me, the weakness is progressing and could continue to worsen, even to the point of total paralysis. Or it could stop well short of that."

"Paralyzed?" he echoed.

"It's only a possibility. You need to understand this so you'll be able to cooperate fully for the next few days in the tests of strength and breathing we'll be doing rather frequently. But nearly everyone recuperates, even in those rare instances when someone so totally loses his ability to swallow and breathe on his own that he needs a respirator."

"A respirator, like when kids got polio?"

Maybe I had gone too far for our first meeting. "Most likely," I said, "you will only get a little weaker. We'll monitor you tonight in the intensive care unit so I can keep a close watch on you." He wasn't listening. His eyes darted about as his thoughts raced.

So I told the couple about the other patients, about eight to ten a year, we had successfully guided through this disease. I left out the rare victim who died from infection or collapse of his blood pressure or who remained forever bound to a wheelchair. And I did not mention Lilly, the forty-eight-year-old woman admitted to the neurology ward at the U.C.L.A. Medical Center who grew so weak that the muscles of her chest wall, arms and legs, diaphragm, vocal cords, and throat became paralyzed. Because she could not blink her eyes, her corneas became inflamed and an ophthalmologist had to sew her eyelids shut. Unable to see, speak, feel, or move, she lay in bed on a respirator for six months.

I was a first-year neurology resident when I took care of Lilly. We knew her mind was working because Guillain-Barré only affects the peripheral nervous system. I'd tell her the time of day, describe the weather and current events, and try to reassure her. But since she could not respond with even a muscle twitch, it was like talking to someone in a coma.

Eighteen months later, nearly back to normal, Lilly returned to the neurology clinic and told me about the bizarre thoughts she'd had during her isolation. Day and night and sleep and wakefulness had grown indistinguishable. She imagined herself floating in space, as if gravity no longer held her down. The voices of doctors, nurses, therapists, and her two teenaged children trickled around her as she swam along the ceiling of her room, bound to earth only by a pliable umbilical tube from the respirator. What people said became bound in ongoing fantasies, especially one about men molesting her. And without any means to communicate for reassurance, she lived in constant fear that some part of her support system was collapsing and that death was imminent. So she counted the regular whooshes of her respirator, up to six thousand breaths over six- to seven-hour intervals, and drifted weightlessly like an astronaut, riding her brain's delusions.

I settled Gallagher in the ICU and checked the breathing capacity of his lungs. He took a deep breath and then exhaled into a mouthpiece connected to a gauge, as if blowing a long note into a clarinet. His lungs emptied four liters of air, a normal amount, so his chest-wall muscles and diaphragm were still strong.

I explained that the fluid we'd draw from a spinal tap might corroborate my diagnosis if it showed a high protein concentration. He agreed to the simple procedure. A nurse turned him on his side and bent his knees into his chest so the knobby spines of his back stood out like those of a frightened cat. I unwrapped a disposable tray of syringes, plastic collection tubes, and gauze, put on sterile gloves, and prepped his lower back. Meticulously, I dipped a sponge on the end of a plastic stick into a well of iodine and drew a spiral over his spiny protuberances from the center out, then repeated this twice with fresh sticks. When the iodine was dry, I numbed the space between the two knobs with a shot of novocaine and quickly passed a three-inch-long needle through the skin, fat, muscle, and ligaments until it popped through the thick tissue that surrounds the spinal fluid. I slowly siphoned off twenty drops of crystal-clear fluid for analysis and pulled out my needle.

I gave the nurses orders to test Dick's limb strength and lung capacity every three hours, even if they had to wake him. If anything worsened or if he began to choke when he swallowed, they were to call me.

On the freeway heading home again, I pulled behind an old VW van with rooftop surf boards and a college sticker on the back window. For a moment, I felt incredibly nostalgic about that annual time of relief when school's out for the summer. Until recently, I had been schooled or trained in a new place every four years—high school in the Philadelphia suburb of Cheltenham, Hamilton College in the tiny upstate–New York town of Clinton, Temple University Medical School in North Philadelphia, internship and finally residency at U.C.L.A. Five years ago, I joined a group of neurologists based in Inglewood, a melting pot, working-class city of one hundred thousand in Los Angeles County. There are now five partners who help cover one another's patients, mostly at the Daniel Freeman Hospital Medical and Rehabilitation Center, a half block from our office, and at the U.C.L.A. Medical Center in Westwood.

The practice has evolved into a good marriage of the medical specialty of neurology, rehabilitation of stroke and head- and spinal-cord-injured patients, teaching U.C.L.A. medical students and residents, and clinical research. And it has halted the rhythms of the peripatetic student's four-year cycle that used to relieve me of serious obligations. Now I had a responsibility to every stranger, like Gallagher, who walked into my life suffering from the terrible things that can happen to ordinary people. But, just like a cop who has seen too much random violence may come to dread a routine check on an errant driver because the motorist could be a gun-toting lunatic, I sometimes barely submerge my desire to avoid new, emotionally threatening encounters.

At home, I bolted down some cold chicken, told Barbara about Dick Gallagher, and went to bed without waking the twins. About midnight, Laura May awakened me with a message she'd mistakenly held for four hours, to see a patient at U.C.L.A.

I phoned the hospital ward. The resident there said a new patient, Dr. Lawrence Oubre, had a brief spell of left-sided weakness and numbness at his office, ignored the symptom, then suffered what seemed to be a stroke with paralysis on the left. But he was stable. His vital signs were normal and he had been alert while his wife visited. It did not sound like an emergency. Then I called the ICU at Freeman, to be sure no one had tried to leave a message about Gallagher. His breathing capacity had dropped a bit, they reported, but he rested comfortably.

By then, my mind had chewed too much for me to sleep, so from the edge of their room I looked in on the twins in their cribs. I remembered how my own parents, when they thought my brother and I were asleep, would stand in the doorway to our room and whisper or muffle a laugh or sometimes simply sigh. I'd melt into a deep sleep in their presence.

Within moments of each other, the twins turned so they lay on their backs across the width of the mattress, one clutching a gray bunny, the other a brown bear. Their chests and bellies seemed to barely fill and empty with each breath. Out of a vague, superstitious premonition, I sat down and rocked in the chair between the cribs. Oubre was well enough to wait until the morning.

TWO

THAT SATURDAY MORNING, only a handful of janitors, nurses, interns, and medical students worked the private patients' floor called the Wilson Pavilion. Weekends always produce a lull in the academic center's heartbeat.

The U.C.L.A. Medical Center, built in the fifties while I was growing up in a brick row house in Philadelphia, has been as important to me in real and perhaps romanticized ways as a child's first friends and playgrounds. Although our neurology practice does the bulk of our consultations for the primary-care physicians at Daniel Freeman—a three-hundred-bed facility with a sixty-bed rehabilitation center run by the Sisters of Saint Joseph of Carondelet—I return to the university's hospital each day as a clinical professor to teach and to consult mostly on patients with a problem related to my special interest, cerebrovascular disease—stroke.

I smiled hello to a resident who once spent a month with us at Freeman on his neurology elective, then pulled Larry Oubre's chart and scanned the notes about the examination and blood tests given him by the admitting resident, intern, and medical student. They agreed that Oubre suffered a stroke, but I detected, between the lines of their scrawled phrases, a touch of self-righteous disbelief. They referred to Oubre as "a P.M.D.," a private medical doctor, by which they meant a practitioner outside their world of academic medicine and, by innuendo, of uncertain training and knowledge. The P.M.D.s of the community, in turn, look upon house staff as inexperienced rookies who are too quick to demean the difficult task real docs have in providing front-line care by themselves But what galled the house staff was that Oubre, a board-certified internist, had ignored the warning signals of his impending stroke. If he couldn't diagnose a garden-variety symptom in himself, how could he have been a good diagnostician for his own patients?

Two days before his admission, Oubre's left arm and leg became numb, as if they had fallen asleep, on at least four occasions. Each spell lasted three to ten minutes. Early yesterday morning, his left leg momentarily collapsed under him and he fell in the bathroom. He took two aspirin, crawled into bed, and went back to sleep. On his way home from work, Oubre lost control of the left side of his body while stopped at a light. Paramedics brought him to the E.R. A computerized scan of the brain, the intern wrote, showed "early signs of an infarction of the right cerebral hemisphere." Oubre's right brain had lost its blood supply. I'd check the x-ray later; first the patient.

A middle-aged woman fluffed the two pillows under Oubre's head, then wiped a streak of saliva from the left side of his chin. He stared off to his right, where three large windows filtered warm morning light across the room. A bag of crystal-clear intravenous fluid dripped slowly through a catheter inserted in his right forearm.

I greeted the couple. Only the woman looked up.

"Oh, yes," she said, but avoided eye contact. "I'm Ethel Oubre. I've been expecting you. My husband's friend and I tried getting you all evening, but your exchange said you weren't taking calls."

I explained the mix-up, but still felt uneasy with the insinuation that I'd shirked my responsibility at a time of need, especially for a fellow physician. Although she would know about the demands made on doctors, her veiled anger differed little from that of anyone who suspected my personal life delayed attendance at the bedside.

At the sound of my voice, Oubre turned his head and eyes far to his right, even though I stood at the left side of his bed. The stroke had apparently damaged the nerve fibers of the pathway for vision that see what's off to the left. They travel from the right half of each retina through the right hemisphere's middle, or parietal lobe, until they reach their primary destination in the visual cortex of the occipital lobe at the far back of the brain. So Oubre viewed the world as if he wore goggles with patches on the left side of each lens. But there was more going on. Oubre wasn't trying to compensate for his visual-field blindness. He did not try to turn his head and eyes to the left in order to focus with the still-functional good half of his vision. Instead, he paid no attention to the environment on his left, as if it did not exist. Searching to find the source of my voice, he slowly pulled out his right hand from under the sheet. I moved to his right side and clasped it. His dark eyes slowly focused on my hand, then scanned up my arm to locate me.

"Bruce, glad you could come," he slurred listlessly. "I've heard a few of your lectures. Believe we've shared a patient or two together." I vaguely recognized him. His face was weary and emotionless. He closed his eyes as if unable to fight off drowsiness.

Oubre's wife nudged him. "Larry, please wake up. Dr. Dobkin needs to talk to you." Turning to me, she added briskly, "He's been like this since I got here an hour ago. You wouldn't have seen him this way last night."

Oubre's lethargy made me suspect that the stroke had caused his right hemisphere to swell. With the devastation caused by a stroke, watery fluids leak out of damaged blood vessels into the surrounding brain tissue. The chemical pumps that ordinarily regulate the flow of water through the porous walls of neurons fail and water rushes in. This fluid can swell a hemisphere downward against the brain stem and compress the neurons that act to keep the brain alert and us conscious. Coaxing him to stay awake, I encouraged Oubre to move his left arm and leg. He could not. When I lifted them and then let go, they dropped like dead things. When I rubbed his skin or wiggled the joints on his left side, he felt nothing.

I looked into his right pupil with my ophthalmoscope. Through this window, I found the head of Oubre's optic nerve. It should have looked like the distinct disc of a summer's setting sun crossed by an X-shaped rivulet of blood vessels. Instead it appeared fuzzy and raised, as if swollen and pushed away from the brain behind it. The pupil suddenly dilated and Oubre slipped further into a barely arousable stupor. I pulled out my pen light and directed its beam into his eye as I had done a few minutes before; this time the pupil did not constrict.

Enormous pressure was building up in the doctor's brain. It had already stretched the nerve to his right pupil, and if it rose any higher in the unexpandable confines of his skull, the intracranial pressure could collapse the thin-walled arteries and veins of both hemispheres and produce widespread destruction of neurons. The only natural pressure-release valve and avenue of escape for Oubre's bulging brain was the outlet called the foramen magnum, a half-dollar-wide opening at the base of the skull where the brain stem joins the spinal cord in the neck. However, if brain tissue coned down through the foramen and herniated against the brain stem, the vital centers that controlled Oubre's blood pressure, breathing, and ultimately life itself would be crushed.

I sent Mrs. Oubre to the waiting room, grabbed Larry's nurse, and ordered mannitol. Within minutes, we were running a thin stream of the clear liquid into his veins. The mannitol acts like an infusion of tiny sponges, which absorb fluid from swollen tissue and then squeeze the excess water into the kidneys for elimination. The only other immediate way to quickly lower Oubre's intracranial pressure was to blow off the carbon dioxide in his lungs by hyperventilating him on a respirator.

This reflexively constricts blood vessels so they take up less space. Then there is more room for the edema fluid, and pressure within the skull falls. The intern arrived and we prepared to intubate Oubre—pass a tube down his throat into his trachea to secure an open airway that we could connect to a respirator for artificial ventilation. But as suddenly as it dilated, his pupil narrowed. The drug had worked. I decided to hold off on intubating the doctor, but we moved him to the intensive care unit for closer monitoring.

Mrs. Oubre waited outside the unit. I lingered there and tried to find something positive to tell her. The build-up of fluid in her husband's damaged brain might continue for another five days. Even an extra tablespoon of water could increase pressure enough to squash his brain down the foramen magnum and either turn him into a machine-dependent vegetable or kill him.

Stalling for a few more minutes, I sat down on one of the beds that occupied each corner of the small ICU. There were the familiar clipboards, charts, telephones, a used syringe, and coffee-stained Styrofoam cups scattered across a long work table in the center of the room. I had practically lived here for two months during my internship in the Department of Medicine. A thoughtful nurse used to keep her transistor radio on a shelf by the window; it was my only connection to the outside world. I've forgotten most of what happened in the news in those days, but the patients stay with me. Oubre rested in the same bed as an Armenian grocer who taught me something important about doctoring.

He was an emaciated, bald, lung-cancer victim in his sixties. His prognosis had always been poor and a chemotherapy side effect had plugged the tiny, fragile air spaces in his lungs with scar tissue so they could not expand even with a forced, deep breath. He was slowly suffocating at home, unable to recline in bed or move more than a few inches without profound air hunger. His mind and senses grew dull, and by the evening of admission, he had slipped into unconsciousness.

As soon as he reached the ICU, we inserted a plastic airway

tube into his trachea and forced pressurized oxygen into his tight chest in order to blow off the carbon dioxide that had built up until it had narcotized his brain. Awakening enough to glare weakly at me, but unable to speak while on the respirator, he wrote on a pad of paper I had offered him, "Let me die." Weeks ago, his wife and daughter had promised him they would not allow medical heroics. Now, our hopeless support exceeded extraordinary measures. He refused to eat or drink.

Three days later, the attending staff physician and I met with the family and their clergyman. The exhausted, delirious patient sat upright with legs crossed and head bowed, refusing to make any comment to his doctors. They asked us to disconnect him from the respirator and to plug the tracheostomy site in his throat so he could talk, and eventually asphyxiate.

I had read an article shortly before the meeting which implied that any Californian can refuse a medical intervention as long as he does not carry an infectious disease or have a dependent child. In the early seventies, there were no legal experts or ethics committees to turn to at U.C.L.A. for advice. What did I understand about agreeing to let my patient die? Medical school had taught me only about trying to prevent death.

I recalled at that moment how my grandfather passed away. He tolerated five heart attacks in the last twenty years of his life, the first on the steps of a trolley car on his way to visit me, his newborn grandson. Harry always recovered quickly and never soured on life. But at age seventy-two, after a surgeon repaired a ruptured aneurysm in his abdomen, he looked feeble. His jowls and shirts hung limply, like features in a caricature of the grand old man I had known. When I visited him during a vacation from college, he told my father and me that he was tired of living. A few weeks later, Harry seemed to recapture some of his remarkable energy and treated his wife and my parents to dinner in a fancy restaurant. On leaving, he asked my mother to drive his car, and on the way home, he closed his eyes and died, as if he had chosen his time.

The grocer's demand reminded me of another incident,

something else that seemed to solidify my moral grounding in this matter. A month before the grocer's admission, I had admitted a thin, stuporous man who took only shallow, gasping breaths. A thick, four-by-four-inch white-gauze patch covered his right eye and cheek. His respiratory distress seemed so great as an intern wheeled him into our unit that I grabbed an intubation tray, spread his gray-blue mouth with a shoehorn-shaped metal laryngoscope, and tried guiding a curved, plastic tube past his vocal cords into his trachea. The anatomy in there was distorted. Suddenly, the gauze patch shimmied and lifted up, pushed out by the bottom of my tube through a crevasse where his eye and cheek used to be. A quarter of his face had been surgically removed. I saw a dime-size, friable, and fleshy growth on an edge of the hole, a remnant of the invading cancer someone tried to extirpate. An odor like spoiled, uncooked chicken arose from the hole and nauseated me. I tried again and slipped the tube into his trachea and hooked him to a respirator.

Minutes later, his wife stormed in and began to scream at me. "Would you want to live looking like that?" she demanded.

I didn't know. "Did he want to live?"

"No," she sobbed. "He started gasping and I panicked and called the paramedics. He'll kill me if he wakes up on a respirator. I promised him no doctor would ever touch him again."

I had batted out of turn, instinctively and wrongly intruding into his process of dying. He never regained consciousness and he died of the pneumonia his wife and I agreed not to treat.

The Armenian grocer had the same right to choose to die as that disfigured patient and my grandfather. Still, I approached his respirator with a light-headed feeling of dissociation, watching for a sign from somebody to stop. The patient unbowed his head. His eyes contacted mine, then penetrated deeper, as if searching for the trigger that would carry me through this ordeal. My finger touched the narrow grooves of the black "off" switch. I pressed and the machine's bellows became silent. Surrounding clatter in the busy unit evaporated.

The grocer's wife and daughter, clothed in black, sat by his side and gently held his arms and hands. The priest stood over them, hands on their shoulders, praying in his vestments. After I buttoned the tracheostomy site, my patient whispered through dry, dusky lips, "This is much better."

Within fifteen minutes he lost consciousness, refusing any struggle to breathe. My neck muscles tightened into a throbbing headache and I barely contained my tears before the weeping family and nurses. I stood at the foot of his bed and watched the monitor of his heart rate slow, then become irregular, and finally stop.

I returned to Ethel Oubre in the waiting room near the ICU. She asked delicately, "How's Larry doing? I know it's bad."

"We caught him just in time. His intracranial pressure's under control for the moment. We'll keep him dry for the next few days and hope his brain swelling doesn't get worse again." I wanted to give her some hope. "Aside from the stroke, he seems in good health. So once he stabilizes, he should do well in a rehabilitation program." I needed to figure out why her husband, only in his early fifties, had had a stroke. "Did Larry describe any other spells of weakness and numbness before three days ago?"

"Not that he told me about."

"Did he complain of headaches or problems with his vision?"

"No, he's perfectly healthy. Never misses a day of work. Never overweight. Played tennis Sundays and golfed a couple of days ago, like every Wednesday afternoon."

I carefully went over Oubre's medical history and habits again, as the house staff had done last night, trying to bring out some piece of information that even a close couple might never have discussed between themselves. Her arms pulled tight across her chest, Mrs. Oubre stared at a nearby gurney and said, "I think Larry took a diuretic for hypertension. He had a bottle of pills I remember seeing in his desk. And he asked me to pick up a bottle of aspirin the day before this happened. But that's all."

Larry's risk for a stroke with untreated high blood pressure would be seven times higher than another man his age who did not have hypertension. Cigarette smoking, high cholesterol and triglycerides, heart disease, and a family history of stroke or heart disease are other risk factors. But Ethel Oubre counted these possibilities out. His grandfather had worked as an overseer on a Louisiana bottomland plantation well into his seventies. His father died, "maybe from a coronary," at seventy-four, but his mother was still active at eighty-three.

"Why do you think he ignored those left-sided attacks? I'd bet he'd have worked up one of his own patients with the same problem."

She sighed. "I guess because he's a doctor and figured he could treat himself. Always does. I mean, he knows himself and makes light of any ache he gets. Having a stroke just isn't something you could see happening to yourself, is it?" She threw back her head and squinted as if tossing down a shot of whiskey. Larry, she realized, probably blew the chance to prevent this catastrophe.

Whatever caused his brief spells of weakness and numbness, so-called transient ischemic attacks, or TIAs, also led to his stroke. The CT scan, as reported, showed no bleeding, so I eliminated the possibility that blood had burst into the brain through the damaged wall of an artery—a cerebral hemorrhage. It seemed more likely that atherosclerosis in either the large right internal carotid artery in his neck or in its major branch on the surface of the brain, the middle cerebral artery, had caused the stroke.

Over years, risk factors like hypertension cause gradual damage to the inner lining of arteries that feed the brain and heart, and they lead to the creation of an atherosclerotic deposit of fat, smooth muscle, blood components, calcium, and other debris. Oubre's TIAs might have occurred either when blood flow briefly slowed on its course through a severely narrowed artery or when some debris broke free from a plaque, traveled upward into a smaller cerebral vessel, and hampered flow for a few minutes. Oubre presumably started taking aspirin because he knew it might help prevent the blood cells called platelets from adhering to a plaque, reducing but not eliminating the risk of a stroke after a warning spell. But when atherosclerosis finally completely plugged his artery, keeping the blood from flowing into much of the right hemisphere for hours, Oubre suffered permanent brain ischemia—a stroke. There was also a chance that a thimbleful of jellylike clot from a damaged heart valve or chamber could have traveled into the brain's branching circulation until it was too large to pass, and plugged an artery. As soon as he was stable, we would search for a cardiac source that might have caused this stroke and could threaten him with yet another.

Mrs. Oubre inquired almost offhandedly, "Will he recover?"

"You mean full recovery?" She nodded as if to say "That's possible, isn't it?" I did not want to exaggerate the point that we were shooting for survival. "He's unlikely to recover much strength on his left side, but if all goes well, his intellect should be fine and perhaps we can get him walking again."

She studied the names of the patients posted in blue marker pen by the door of the ICU. "I know you'll do everything possible."

I promised to return after finishing my rounds here and at Freeman. The house staff would call me if anything changed. Then I walked to the radiology department to check Larry's CT scan.

The scanner produces images of the brain as if it were sliced like a loaf of bread in consecutive horizontal cuts parallel to the plane between the ear drums and corners of the eyes. A computer creates these images based on how much of the beam of x-rays is absorbed by brain matter, spinal fluid, and diseased tissue, each having a different density. Oubre's left hemisphere showed the peppery gray shades of normal brain structures. On each cut, however, a dark shadow like an eclipse had moved across over two-thirds of the right side of his brain. When the scan was taken, the edema had not yet spread enough to show itself pushing against the rest of the brain. But within that shadow lay dying neurons and cut pathways that were responsible for Oubre's inability to move, feel, and perceive. And no medication or surgery could reverse the death of half of Larry's brain.

In the ICU at Freeman, Dick Gallagher leaned back in his bed reading the *Los Angeles Times* sports section. Glass partitions separated him from the ten other patients whose beds semicircled the central nurse's station with its cardiac-rhythm monitors. A warbling murmur of electronics and voices drifted softly into the Gallagher cubicle. His wife and parents were seated in chairs on both sides of the yellow bedspread crumpled at his feet. Tanned and hirsute, with a weekend weightlifter's arms and chest, Dick hardly looked ill. But then I noticed how he slid his forearm across his lap to turn a page, unable without great effort to raise it against gravity.

"How's it going?"

"Okay," he said and introduced me to the family. His mother, the source of Dick's blue-gray eyes, and the father, from whom Dick inherited his thick black hair, offered me a plate of homemade chocolate-chip cookies and a bowl of fruit.

"Did you sleep in some this morning?" Sharon asked. Dick's father cleared his throat.

"Got tied up at U.C.L.A. with a colleague who suffered a severe stroke."

"Will he be all right?" the wife and mother asked simultaneously.

"Don't know yet. How was your night?" I asked Dick as I pulled out my reflex hammer.

"Couldn't sleep much. I guess the lung-capacity tests freaked me out. The nurse kept saying to try harder when my numbers fell, but I was blowing out my guts. And then the guy next to me, a real old fellow, must've turned bad because they were trying to resuscitate him around four. Someone said he stopped breathing." The bed was empty now.

The amount of air Dick exhaled from his lungs had dropped from 4 liters on admission to 3.2 last night and was down to 2.6

this morning. It was still in a safe range, but this was an ominous trend. He had lost the tendon reflexes in his arms. His toes and ankles were now paralyzed, and I overcame the resistance of the rest of his arm and leg muscles with the strength of two of my fingers. Walking was now impossible. Feeling in his hands and feet was still muffled, but at least this loss had not come to involve more of his limbs.

Dick looked at his father with a half smile and said, "Guess I'm not going home today."

His parents fired questions at me from a list his mother held. Could the insecticide that Dick sprayed in his garage a few months ago—that nasty-smelling stuff that gave him a rash—cause this? They kept a cat in the house for a neighbor six months ago that later became ill and died. Could he have picked up something from the animal? Did he catch something out at Joshua Tree? And, most important, was this contagious?

I explained that the high concentration of protein and absence of white cells in Dick's spinal fluid helped to confirm that he suffered with the Guillain-Barré syndrome. The disease was not transmissible or likely to result from any of the sources they suggested. I'd test his blood for some of the common viruses that are thought to be capable of instigating the disease, but even if Sharon had been exposed to the same virus as her husband, the odds were greatly against her also getting Guillain-Barré. Dick's illness rose from an aberration in what are still obscure immunological processes. A virus stirred up his blood's white cells to defend against infection. These circulating cells produced antibodies and other substances that neutralized the virus but, in error, also attacked the insulation, called myelin, that protectively covers peripheral nerves.

I laid out our options. I could start him on steroids, which might suppress the immunologic reaction. The drug posed several immediate potential complications, which included increasing Dick's susceptibility to serious infection and the rare, long-term potential for relapse as we tapered off the steroids.

We could try plasmapheresis, a kind of bloodletting in which a catheter similar to ones used in kidney dialysis continuously draws blood into a machine that separates its various components, removes a percentage of all the antibodies present, and recirculates the "cleaned" blood. Infection, protein depletion, and a sharp drop in blood pressure leading to temporary shock could complicate the procedure. I did not mention that we already sent one Guillain-Barré patient off to neurosurgery to remove a brain abscess that developed after plasmapheresis lowered his defenses against infection. The surgeon had to open the back of the man's skull and cut and suction out three tablespoonfuls of pus, leaving the patient without vision on his left side.

While some neurologists swore by the efficacy of steroids or the mechanical leech, no one had yet accumulated enough information to be able to say whether either therapy clearly decreased the duration and severity of an attack or improved the chance for full recovery. I had recently talked to a neurologist at the University of Pennsylvania who was participating in a controlled trial aimed at determining the usefulness of plasmapheresis. The answer, he said, was still over a year away. Giving Dick general support and vitamins for nerve regrowth might be safer and as effective as any experimental treatment.

I suggested that we wait another day to see if Dick's weakness might stabilize on its own. While his family patiently attended an invisible struggle between immune cells and nerve fibers, I began my rounds.

Our neurology group had consulted on several other patients in the ICU. Alphretta Wells, a nearly blind diabetic who had been on kidney dialysis since she turned sixty-seven and had spent the past year in a nursing home because she had become too confused to live alone, was being treated for pneumonia and a stroke. Two elderly women on respirators were in comas caused by liver or kidney failure. A priest in his eighties also suffered from organ failures when he was resuscitated too late after his heart stopped beating. None of the patients could speak or hear, so I examined them quickly, checked their lab data, and made a few suggestions to their primary docs. I urged the priest's physician to withhold treatments for infections or another cardiac arrest, if his family agreed, since there was no chance of recovery of higher brain function. I would have given the same advice to the doctors of the other patients, but they seemed intent on aggressive treatment of these almost certainly terminal diseases. Medicine like this disillusions me.

On other floors, I followed up on patients with pinched neck or low-back nerves who were responding to medication and bed rest, a women in her thirties whose balance and vision had suddenly deteriorated from a bout of multiple sclerosis, and others with strokes, head injuries, dementia, malignant tumors of the brain or spinal cord, and symptoms without clear causes yet. Then I rechecked Gallagher.

Only four hours since I last examined him, his strength and breathing capacity had dwindled slightly again. I asked, "Think you'll be able to sleep tonight?"

He raised his shoulders and crossed his wrists as if confined by a straitjacket. "I think I'm afraid I might stop breathing if I close my eyes. What about a sleeping pill?"

"No. It could depress your breathing. Try to relax."

"Yeah. Relax. Jeez, I'm even afraid to let my kids see me like this. The boy's only five and our girl's three. You just never believe anything like this could happen." He riveted his eyes on mine. "I could stay crippled or die from this, huh?" Tears filled the corners of his eyes.

"No, that's very unlikely nowadays. We just have to wait out the disease and avoid complications. And don't worry about the kids. They'll accept anything as long as they can see and touch you."

"I guess I can't stand doing nothing. I need to fight this. Let's go for the bloodletting."

"Okay. I'll arrange for plasmapheresis in the morning if you're not better. Remember, it may be as effective as witchcraft." He laughed as I sat down on the edge of his bed. "It's not easy being a father, is it?"

"I dunno. Sharon can always take care of herself. With kids, if anything happens, it's a lot tougher. You got any?"

"Identical twin daughters, only a year old."

"Enjoy every stage. They grow fast."

I wanted to do that, but I had to see Oubre first.

At U.C.L.A., the doctor's wife was smoothing his sheets under his chin as I entered. Alert, though still vigilant only to his right, he held out his hand to shake mine. His mouth was too dry to speak above a whisper. His right pupil was larger again and a bit sluggish in its light reflex. More intracranial pressure was building. Despite wanting to restrict his fluid intake so his brain would have less water to sop up, I offered him a half ounce of ice chips to swish in his caked mouth.

"So how's it going? Did you get in any golf today?" he whispered coarsely as I bent my ear to him.

"Never liked golf, but I see you didn't do any better."

"Maybe in a few days."

"Give me at least a coupla weeks to get you in shape."

He closed his eyes and I reassured his wife that our holding pattern was a good sign. Then I tracked down the intern covering him that night.

"Oubre's getting too much intravenous fluid. I wanted fifty cc.'s an hour of straight saline and he's up to seventy-five of dextrose and half-normal saline," I charged.

"We felt he was getting too dry. His urine output dropped and his BUN bumped up," he said defensively. A rise in the BUN—blood's urea nitrogen—meant that Oubre might become too dehydrated for his kidneys to filter his blood.

I told him about the change in the doctor's eyes and he listened intently as I laid out an overnight game plan.

At home that Saturday evening, a few phone calls of no consequence interrupted my first chance in two days to talk to my wife and play with the babies. When I called at ten, Oubre's nurses reported that his pupils were normal again, and Gallagher's said he was stable. I went to sleep. Then, at 5:00 A.M., Oubre's intern called to tell me that his patient's right pupil had fully dilated and did not constrict even after he pumped in more dehydrating agents. The doctor awakened momentarily when pinched, but not when called.

"Get him on a respirator and blow off his carbon dioxide to

around twenty-five," I said, barely awake. "And run the mannitol continuously. I'll be there in a half hour."

My mind reworked the case against the ceiling of my darkened bedroom. Something did not fit. Why such malignant cerebral edema?

I shaved and dressed, while in the ICU the house staff pushed drugs. The phone rang again. Barbara wearily handed me the receiver and was asleep by the time I carried it into the bathroom. I half expected to hear an anonymous voice tell me the doctor had died. But it was Gallagher's night nurse informing me that his breathing capacity had dropped to 2.1 liters. If it fell any lower, I would have to put a tube into *his* trachea, too, and ventilate him on a respirator before his weakness caused respiratory failure. I pulled an article from my files about an experimental treatment using barbiturates for massive cerebral edema and left the house.

Oubre's bed in the ICU was empty. My pulse pounding in my throat, I turned to a nurse sitting by the work table and asked what happened to the patient in Bed 2. She had just come on this shift. She didn't know.

The intern who called me trudged in, looking tired in his blood-smudged white pants and green scrub shirt. "We moved Oubre to the unit across the hall. There's more room for a respirator."

"Jesus, did you scare me. How's he doing?"

"He's kinda stable, but gorked out. BUN's up to forty, osmolality's up to three hundred twenty, but the blood pressure's fine. And he spiked a temperature. Blood gases are good on thirty-percent oxygen with the carbon dioxide at twenty-five." So his body was very dry and his lungs were well-ventilated. But the fever could add to his intracranial pressure.

Our only gauge of fluctuations in Larry's intracranial pressure derived from examining his alertness, eye and pupillary movements, strength, and reflexes. Oubre did not greet me at the bedside. He made no response to my voice and only reflexively extended his left arm and leg when I rubbed his chest.

His right eye barely rotated side to side in its socket, and the left one no longer turned out, suggesting that the boggy brain squatted on the cranial nerves to the eye muscles as they passed from the brain stem on their way to the bone of the orbits. Even his right arm and leg now showed abnormal reflexes. So Oubre's brain stem was feeling the downward pressure from his right hemisphere. We were very close to a total collapse of brain-stem function.

"His intracranial pressure's too high. Let's wrap him in a cooling blanket to bring down his temp and get him drier," I mumbled more to myself than to the intern who had miscalculated how badly things were going. A young doctor's ego knows no bounds until he has been burned by his inexperience a few times. "You must pay closer attention to his exam or he'll die in perfect chemical balance."

"He can't get much more dehydrated or we'll get into acute renal failure," he protested.

"It's the only hope. We'll push up his blood pressure a bit with drugs to help keep up his cerebral blood flow. The hell with his kidneys for now. We've got to buy him at least forty-eight hours."

We agreed on a plan for infusing several anti-edema agents, depending on Oubre's response. I was already going beyond any regimen I had ever needed before, and I was hardly a novice in these matters. I told the intern we were on an uncharted course, but that he'd learn every practical trick in controlling cerebral edema by the time we finished.

The alternatives were especially risky. A neurosurgeon could, in an act of desperation, cut out some of Oubre's dead right hemisphere to make room for what was left. When he opened the skull, the boggy brain under pressure would ooze up and drool out. Only a rare stroke victim survived this measure with any long-term quality of life. Or we might start Oubre on an experimental drug treatment with barbiturates. In doses that anesthetize the patient, barbs can sometimes lower intracranial pressure. But we would need a neurosurgeon to implant a pressure gauge through his skull into the space around the brain to monitor the effects of the drug, and gauges are not always reliable. Plus, Oubre's heart and blood pressure might falter under the stress of anesthesia.

At Freeman, Dick Gallagher greeted me with a resigned expression. "I think I'm a little worse. Can we get your leeches?"

"The pathologists should be here by nine for your first pheresis. It takes them a while to get out of bed on a Sunday."

"I thought pathologists did autopsies, like Quincy. You're not trying to tell me something?"

"No. According to the EKG monitor, your heart is still beating and therefore you are alive."

"Thanks for the diagnosis. But aren't I weaker?" he asked, chewing on his lower lip. He could no longer even slide his arms or legs across the bed sheets, though he breathed easily. I nodded.

"If I get through this, Bruce, the first thing I do is take my wife out dancing. She's always bugging me to go. I don't care how silly I look."

"Let's not make rash promises under duress. I'll see you before I leave, whenever that is."

Four new hospital consultations, rounds, and several calls from outpatients detained me until six, well after Dick completed his first pheresis. He became a little shocky when the pathologist drained off too much plasma, but his blood pressure returned to normal with a quick infusion of saline and albumin.

"I'm cleaner and meaner." He grinned. His wife spoon-fed him mashed potatoes, leaving a mustache of gravy.

"Then we'll homogenize your plasma again in the morning."

"When will you be able to promise that I won't have to go on a respirator?" he asked.

"Your breathing capacity hasn't changed in twelve hours. If everything stays stable for four to five days, or begins to improve, you've got it made. But getting the strength to walk may not come back for weeks or months, even if you stabilize now."

"Boy, would I like to scratch and feed myself."

"Hey, aren't I being a good nurse?" asked his wife. Dick turned his head and tried moving toward her, but his dead body-weight anchored him.

I stopped by the U.C.L.A. unit on my way home. The intern had called around one to say that Oubre seemed more easily arousable. His wife slumped in a high-backed, green-padded chair by the door. Her son, a gawky teenager with tightly curled black hair, sat on the chair's wooden arm, his hand on her sloped shoulder. They nodded a hello and let me pass when I promised to talk after checking Larry.

After somewhat churlishly demanding to know who I was, his nurse, a stocky young woman with a buttery face, offhandedly mentioned that Oubre kept asking for a soda. She must be referring to someone else, I thought, as I reached his side. But there he sat, shaved, groomed, and wearing a fresh white scrub shirt, showing only a trace of his haggard, moribund countenance from the morning. I called his name, and to my amazement, he searched off to his right for me and held out his right hand until I grasped it. His abnormal eye signs had nearly cleared. Unable to talk with the endotracheal tube jammed down his throat, he communicated by scrawling requests or answers to questions with a single word on a note pad. I told him that we had his cerebral edema under reasonable control and he wrote "OK."

His lab values still concerned me; we had more of those spongy molecules slurping up brain water than I imagined safe. Yet his blood pressure and kidneys held steady. Both Oubre and Gallagher seemed blessed. I wrote a note in Oubre's chart commending the house staff and urged them not to alter the regimen.

"His improvement is dramatic," I reported to Oubre's wife and son. "He's not completely out of danger, but our juggling act has worked."

She squeezed her son's arm and said, "Thank God. But when will he be out of danger?"

"I'm not sure. It's so unusual to herniate as rapidly as he did and then respond so well to the anti-edema drugs. We'll start judiciously increasing his fluids in several days and then get him off the respirator if he's stable. I discussed the case with one of the staff neurosurgeons. He did not want to intervene. And that seems to have worked out for the best."

I drove home and fell into bed after dinner and a few love messages from Laura May. But at six on Monday morning, an anonymous voice from the answering service called.

"The ICU told me to let you know that your patient died at four A.M." Even more cryptically, the unidentifiable voice went on, "She said not to wake you since you probably expected it."

"Died. Oubre died?" I asked in disbelief. "With all the crap nurses call me about they told you to hold this?"

"She didn't give me the name."

"You don't know who died?" Was I dreaming? "Wait a minute. Which ICU?"

"The call came in at four-ten from . . . let me check what's written here . . . from Daniel Freeman ICU."

"Gallagher?" My mind went instantly hyperalert. I should have intubated him. How could I let him die of respiratory failure? Or maybe his blood pressure and heart rate bottomed out. In some Guillain-Barré victims, the peripheral autonomic nerves spill their neurotransmitter, norepinephrine, which can strain the heart into failure. But the nurses knew what warning signs to look for. If they told me, I could have treated it. They probably called old Jake Springstein instead.

"The nurse did not say who it was and we do not ask. We only convey messages."

Why is this woman tormenting me? Where's Laura May?

I phoned the ICU. Dick was eating breakfast. Alphretta Wells, blind and senile, had mercifully died.

THREE

AS I PULLED OUT of the doctors' parking lot at Freeman, I saw a youngster in the school yard across the street slam a basketball over the head of another child, knocking him to the ground. I stopped my car, but by the time I got out, they were off and running. Then, on the drive up to U.C.L.A., an accident I hadn't thought about in twenty-five years came to mind. I had been sitting on the pavement of a back alley with a half-dozen kids, waiting for my turn to bat in a game of stickball. Suddenly, the top of my head became warm and spongy and ached. A liquid trickled into my ears and down my neck as if someone were slowly pouring it onto my scalp. My father hadn't been there what seemed like a moment before, but now he squatted next to me. As he pulled off his shirt and pressed it against my head, he said that everything would be okay. I could not speak or cry.

He cradled me in his arms, lifted me, and walked through a crowd with his shirt cloth still pressed into the warm mush on my head. His face was painfully tense, but his voice and grip reassured me that he knew precisely what had to be done. It was only years later, during one of our summer drives home from work, that I learned he had been a medic. The army, in its frantic wisdom in December 1942, threw him into their Medical Corps because he had managed a drugstore before he enlisted, and they figured he could at least read prescriptions. That was all I knew. He would never talk about his experiences during the war.

Larry Oubre sat propped up in his bed when I visited on Tuesday evening. His lips were desiccated and split despite the greasy petrolatum used to moisten them. He wore a wet towel wrapped around his head like a turban, and from the left corner of his mouth the pale blue endotracheal tube hung like an opium smoker's water pipe. Larry looked drugged—and he probably was.

The body synthesizes its own opiates, called endorphins. These chemicals locate and dock on the walls of neurons at specialized receptors, like ships pulling into the slips of a wharf. Each nerve cell responds only to the chemical neurotransmitters that fit *precisely* into its wharfs. Any drug that alters mental function acts like a messenger that excites, inhibits, or modulates the neurons that receive it. Receiving neurons even adjust the number of receptors in their walls, so they apparently can vary how much they'll be influenced. Oubre languished in bed as if shiploads of Valium, morphine, and whiskey had docked in his slips.

When I called his name, Larry's eyes made slow searching movements up and down the right side of his yellow ribbed bedspread. Then he stretched out his hand until I grasped it and we held our handshake. I asked if he needed anything. On his note pad, he slowly scribbled "Orange Crush." Once free of the respirator, I said, he could look forward to a case of soda from me. I put my other hand on his shoulder and promised we'd try to extubate him tomorrow.

I don't often see doctors touch their patients as a sign of support and sympathy. I had to learn that this is an important part of doctoring. Before starting medical school, what I knew about physicians at work derived from the television melodramas of Kildare and Casey and from Dr. Arthur Krieger, my family physician, to whom I went for an occasional inspection and injection. By the time I was seven, he handed me an anatomy book whenever I waited in his office. I grew fascinated by the pictures of organs and the polysyllabic words. Krieger had delivered me, amniotic wet and dazed; maybe I looked like a potential medical student. From my liberal-arts view on Hamilton College's isolated hill, doctoring seemed to embrace what the sixties incited in me—social goodness, moral certainty, and an escape from the madness of the war in Vietnam. The first two years at Temple University's School of Medicine required only the sort of commitment I'd make to learn to read and become conversant in a foreign language. It wasn't until the third year, with its hospital-ward rotations, that I began to realize what the practice of medicine was all about.

One of my first patients was a wistful high-school senior only a few years younger than a recent date had been. A faded gold nightshirt, the same shade as her hair, covered her down to mid-thigh, making her seem more wholesome than sexy, especially with her frumpled, grayed-brown teddy bear watching us from a bedside table. She reticently described the progressive, painful hardening of her breasts over the last several months; each breast was cancerous, and she was here at the university hospital for chemotherapy.

Awkwardly, I examined her neck, chest, back, and limbs by listening with stethoscope, tapping, and palpating. My movements were still too new to be fluid. To get to her abdomen, I fumbled with the nightshirt until it pulled free from under her buttocks, then slid the bed sheet up over her exposed groin to preserve our modesty. But as I leaned forward, the pens, flashlight, calipers, and cards from the breast pocket of my first white coat spilled out onto her belly. She tried not to giggle but couldn't restrain herself, and I laughed, too, wanting to believe this healthy-looking young woman wasn't dying. Then I examined her breasts. They rested like wetted molds of sand bound in thinly stretched velvet. I could neither sway nor depress them. I felt the same queasy jitters I had every time I kneeled in the starting blocks before a 440-yard hurdles race in college.

"I guess you get your first intravenous medication this afternoon," I said in a parched murmur. She nodded and a few moments passed. "Would you like me to get you ice cream or a hoagie before I leave tonight?"

"They say I'll be nauseated," she replied, as if annoyed by a trivial eventuality. A resident had described the intravenous nitrogen mustard she would get as a vile liquefied nerve gas that induced violent retching.

"I'll come back anyway. I can tell your folks about a nearby seafood restaurant they can take out food from, if you feel up to clams and stuff later." That was the best I could offer. Hands deep in the side pockets of my white jacket, I felt more like an ice-cream truck driver than a soon-to-be physician.

Chemotherapy might prolong her life a few months, but she deserved a cure, not just a few days bought with toxic patchwork that would turn her stomach, denude her scalp of hair, and expose her to infections that antibiotics could not expunge. It seemed impossible to me that doctors did not have something better; they were healers. But the science of medicine was almost useless here. And I felt remarkably unprepared for the emotional intricacies of serious illness, suffering, and dying. Perhaps like my baby-boom generation, trained after doctors had treatments for polio, fulminating infections, and organ failures, and after the ubiquitous shelter of nursing homes blinded us to the elderly and invalid, I had lost touch with the naturalness of disease and death.

And then that teenager taught me a lesson that has become a part of me. She asked me to sit down with her whenever I spoke to her, and to hold her hand. Seated, eye-to-eye, touching, we shared her fears. That was also the best medicine I could offer Larry Oubre that day.

The next morning, we took Oubre off the respirator and re-

moved his endotracheal tube. The doctor still looked as dopey
as a nodding-out heroin addict, but he was alert enough to
swallow sips of water and pureed food. His voice was little more
than a raspy whisper, partly because the tube had irritated his
vocal cords and perhaps from weakness the stroke caused to the
muscles of the left side of his larynx. I phoned Mrs. Oubre at
her home.

"Thank God we're past the critical stage." She sighed. "Can
you move him out of intensive care? There's so much commo-
tion there."

"I'd like to keep him under close observation two more days.
The CT scan we repeated yesterday showed quite a bit of
swelling in his right hemisphere." The bottom and inner border of his right temporal lobe, the banana-shaped lobe that
nestles like a thumb against each hemisphere's fist, was jutting
threateningly close to Oubre's brain stem. "So we have to be
careful," I continued. "But I'm real hopeful. In a few days we'll
hydrate him up and, in a week, transfer him to the rehabilitation center at Daniel Freeman."

"He's not out of the woods," she muttered, as if reporting to
someone by her side.

"Almost," I encouraged. "Could you pick up a few cans of
Orange Crush? I promised Larry a ration." She laughed.

When I arrived in the ICU at Freeman, Dick Gallagher was
hooked up for his third plasmapheresis in four days. His peripheral-nerve damage had progressed despite the treatments,
and now he could not even twitch the muscles in his arms and
legs. Fortunately, his chest wall and diaphragm expanded suf-
ficiently to take enough air into his lungs, and he could swallow
without choking. Three times a day I pondered over his lab
values with a pulmonary consultant, and each time we opted to
hold off on mechanical support. But the brief scare and soul-
searching from two mornings ago when my answering-service
operator led me to imagine Dick died from respiratory failure
hung over me.

I had done Gallagher's nerve-conduction studies on Monday. I administered a small electric shock to two points along peripheral nerves just under the skin of his arm and leg. The jolt made his thumb or toes twitch, allowing me to calculate the speed with which his own electrochemical impulses traveled along his nerves. The test showed profound slowing of the few nerve fibers that still worked at all: clear signs of a severe Guillain-Barré syndrome. The systems in his brain that coordinated his ability to move could order the motor neurons in the spinal cord to fire the muscles they were connected to, but no messages could pass the roadblocks of inflammation in his peripheral-nerve highways. His peripheral cranial nerves were not completely spared either, evidenced by the persistent mild weakness of his face and his nasal voice. But these nerves behaved more like highways with large potholes that could be detoured. He was paralyzed from the neck down, and yet he was by far the most medically fit and stable of any patient in that unit.

"So," he asked, "you like my tubes?"

"They're my tubes," injected the cherubic pathologist from behind the pheresis unit, a modern sculpture of flywheels, coils, and blood-cell separators. "It's only your blood."

"The hocus-pocus continues with our up-to-date leeching process, I see. How do you feel?"

"Feel? I'm lying here like a deer with four busted legs in an open field." He quickly regained control. "Oh, I'm all right. No better, but at least I'm not getting light-headed and sweaty like I did on Sunday when Dr. Vampire first struck."

"You're holding your own, which is what we need. Real improvement may take a while."

"I'll take anything positive. Now if you could tell me when I'll be able to take a dump on a toilet instead of a bedpan, I'd be grateful."

"Soon. Are your hands and feet still tingling?" I asked.

"They're kinda burning, worse than yesterday, I think. It's such a weird feeling. Fluctuates like they're asleep or hot, sometimes like pins and needles. Does it mean the nerves are growing back?"

"It's called a dysesthesia, a sort of noisy static from the injured nerves which your brain perceives as a message of discomfort. In a way, it's like the feeling you'd get from whacking the nerve at your elbow. You know, your funny bone."

"So it's nothing . . . I mean, nothing about getting better?"

"Look, I'd bet the disease has gotten as bad as it will. You've peaked. We'll stop the plasma exchanges after tomorrow's," I added, with a consoling glance at the astounded-looking pathologist. He would pherese a patient for a week or more, although we had no good data yet about effectiveness and safety of the procedure. I had no objective way to assess it, so I decided not to push my luck and cause a serious complication. "In a day or two, you'll be out of the unit to a regular room, and then to rehab."

That night, I was on call again to cover emergencies for my group. As I sat down to dinner, Harold Boeing's nursing aide dutifully called to report that he had fallen on top of Harold— a recently discharged stroke patient—while assisting him off the toilet at home.

"Is he hurt?" I asked.

"No, no," answered the aide. "He's fine."

"Then why are you calling?"

"Just thought you should know. His wife was worried."

With my salad, a nurse called to ask if Mrs. Johnstone could take the vitamin C tablets she had brought from home.

"Does she need it tonight? Couldn't someone ask when her doctor ordinarily sees her?"

"She says she forgets to ask."

I knew an internist who ripped the phone out of the wall during an evening full of vacuous interruptions. As I returned to my congealed lamb chops and cold green beans and carrots, the high drama of modern medicine peaked.

"This is John Price, R.N., on Two East," announced a formal, unmistakable high-pitched voice that had plagued me nearly every night when on call. "Mr. T. Crenshaw would like something for pain."

"Who is T. Crenshaw, John Price, R.N.?"

"He's a patient admitted for low-back pain. His present pain is in his low back. Sciatica, I believe."

"Sounds like a most unusual problem to contemplate while I'm eating dinner. Whose patient is he?"

"Dr. Ludwig saw him." Ludwig, one of my partners, mentioned that he had evaluated someone with a slipped disc that pinched the fifth lumbar nerve and caused severe pain and leg weakness. Crenshaw would have back surgery for the herniated disc within the next two days.

"He must have had medication ordered for control of pain. Who's his primary doctor?"

"Drs. Darcy, Prairy, and Axmunster."

"Why not ask one of them for medication? We're the consultants."

"They don't answer their pages."

Whoever was on call wanted to finish his dinner. "What was ordered for pain?" I asked with mounting annoyance.

"Aspirin and sixty milligrams of codeine."

"Does that help?"

"Yes. But he wants it now so he can sleep and it's ordered every four hours. Only three hours have passed since the last pill, so I told him I'd have to wake him if he fell asleep."

"Wake him? Give it now so he can fall asleep."

"Very good."

As I hung up, Barbara asked, "Is it my turn yet?"

"You wouldn't believe this nurse. He's stringing out some poor guy in pain who only wants enough relief to fall asleep. How are things?" I gobbled my cold food and tried to relax into Barbara's description of her ballet class and the shenanigans of our girls.

The next call interrupted a hot shower. Barbara sympathetically echoed the operator's words. "Dr. Dobkin. Mr. Cannery is afraid he's having a stroke. Will you speak to him?"

With a towel around my waist, I answered the emergency. "Hello, Dr. Orfuss?" asked a deep voice.

"This is Dr. Dobkin, covering for Orfuss. Can I help you?"

"Well, I'm Dr. Orfuss's patient. He said to call him if any new symptoms came up. Guess I can talk to you instead." You don't have to, I thought.

"I've got this twitch in my left eye."

"Your eyelid is twitching?"

"Thought it might be a little stroke. They called it a TIA last time. My right arm got numb and clumsy, but the tests didn't show any blood-artery blockages."

"And now the lower lid is flickering?" I guessed, as water dripped into my ear and down my neck.

"Yeah. How did you know?"

"Does anything else twitch or feel weak or numb?"

He hesitated, as if pinching his limbs. "No, everything's fine."

I explained, "It's just a fasciculation, some irritable muscle fibers. It happens to everybody, especially with fatigue or anxiety. The twitching has nothing to do with a warning of stroke."

"Oh, good. I am tired. G'night."

"Good night." Aesculapius must have had it in for me.

Barbara estimates the necessity of these intrusions by rating my glower as I listen to the nurse or patient calling. It wasn't until a problem arose with her pregnancy that I realized how sensitized she had become to my barely contained anger with nonsense calls. Near delivery, she sat in pain for an entire night without telling me, while our twins kicked frantically and I slept. In the morning, she explained that she had not wanted to disturb her obstetrician that late. I was self-righteously furious.

"He's a doctor," I insisted. "He's supposed to answer his patients any time of day. If you suspect something's wrong, you call."

I was filled with terrifying images of brain-damaged children. And it turned out that our babies were in even more distress than I. When the obstetrician delivered them by Caesarean section a few hours later, their twisted, nearly bloodless umbilical cords were wrapped around their five-pound bodies. He unpacked and lifted each blue and breathless infant. After the longest moments of my life, each cried, then stretched and flexed her arms in a Moro's reflex, like perfect wonders of procreation. That day's fear has mitigated my impatience with the often senseless anxieties of night callers.

A continuous ring startled me from the kind of restless and dream-filled sleep that accompanies nights on call. I punched the clock-radio's snooze alarm; the ringing persisted. I reached for the phone and placed the earpiece at my mouth. The digitalized time read 2:17 A.M. For an instant, as I flipped the receiver to my ear, I feared that something had happened again to my father. But a Muzak voice toned, "Dr. Dobkin, I hope I didn't disturb you. I have the ICU at Daniel Freeman on the line. Shall I put them through?"

"Laura May, if this is a nurse waking me for a sleeping-pill order, I'll cut someone's frontal lobes. What are you doing on the night shift, anyway?"

Barbara breathed something about keeping the noise down.

"Just trying to pay the bills like everyone else. Here's the ICU."

"Hello, Dr. Dobkin? It's Dr. Jack Frankfort here," he began rather formally. "I've got this sixty-year-old black male 'found down.' No responses, even to noxious stimulation." I could have predicted Frankfort's examination technique. He pinched the victim's nipples, maybe even his testicles, and squashed a nail bed on each hand and foot to try to stimulate movement. The more subtle aspects of a neurological exam were usually omitted by internists.

Frankfort added, "No metabolic problems, no cardiac history or trauma. Could you see him tonight? Don't know what's going on."

"I'll be right over," I said with false goodwill.

"Appreciate it. I'm leaving, so order whatever you want."

As the garage door opened, the spicy fragrance from nearby white-flowering-jasmine shrubs lessened my feeling of harassment. During my training at U.C.L.A., I secretly relished chances to test my stuff when no one else was nearby to bail me out. It was my trial by ordeal. And my haggard face at rounds the next morning proclaimed my rite of sacrifice to peers, professors, and nurses. House staff find perverse consolation in looking ragged. As I pulled the car onto the freeway, I recalled one of those nights I had marched with a measure of bravado down an empty, poorly lit corridor at 3:00 A.M. toward an anxious intern who was unable to control the seizures of an epileptic in the E.R. I felt like Gary Cooper in *High Noon*. The theme song from *The Magnificent Seven* played in my mind; I reached for my stethoscope, twirled it by the earpieces, and promptly whacked myself in the jaw.

Tonight, the second-floor hallway at Freeman was empty, except for one nurse hurrying to a room with a lighted "call" signal over its door. A few yards away from the ICU, behind the waiting room's glass partition, a dozen men and women, all black, talked as if sitting on their porch on a hot afternoon. Inside the unit, a wide-awake nurse, too bouncy for my mood, handed me the patient's chart. Dick Gallagher slept two cubicles away from the new consultation.

According to meager notes, Moses Abraham Johnson was sixty-four with a history of angina and poorly controlled hypertension. At 10:00 P.M., while with his family, he suddenly slumped in his chair. Paramedics brought him to the E.R. and the physician here intubated Johnson because his breathing was too shallow. They had waited for the results of a CT scan of the brain and blood tests before calling me. These revealed no cause for the patient's state. The electrocardiogram and vital signs were normal, except for a blood pressure of 180/110. The only other available information was that he was unemployed and on Medicaid, which would pay my neurology group about forty dollars for the night's work.

I pulled Johnson's covers down and began my routine. Any annoyance I had felt at being called out of bed faded as I examined him, replaced by a compelling bond, an automatic social contract that forms between even an unconscious patient and me. This intimacy never evolves so quickly and firmly with people I meet outside the mantle of medicine.

Johnson, a muscular six-footer with a laborer's calluses at the base of his toes and fingers, had the unwrinkled face of a much younger man. His eyelids were half-open, but his eyes were immobile and blank. A respirator breathed regularly for him. He made no response when I called his name, touched his face, moved a finger as if threatening to poke his eye, jiggled his arms and legs, or pressed my thumb deep into the flesh of his hands and feet. His pupils constricted to my pen light's glare, but that seemed to be the only sign of brain activity. He did not even have any tendon reflexes. As all the possible explanations for his seemingly unconscious state ran through my mind, I thought I saw him blink. So I held one finger before his face and asked him to blink once. His eyelids stayed half-closed. I said, "Moses, try to close and open your eyes."

A second or two passed, then he blinked.

"Blink three times," I said excitedly. He slowly opened and closed his lids three times, without a twitch from his other facial muscles.

"Try and do what I say. Blink once if the answer to a question is yes, and twice if the answer is no. Is your name Moses?"

His partly opened lids closed once.

"Are you thirty years old?"

His dark brown eyes looked more alive. He blinked twice.

"Are you sixty-four?"

One blink.

"Can you wiggle your fingers or toes?"

No response. I raised his hand so he could see it. "Can you feel me move these fingers?"

One blink. Our coded communication disclosed that he knew what day it was, felt no pain, and wanted to see his wife. I explained the neurologic disability to Johnson and his nurse, then headed for the waiting room, suppressing a yawn despite the exhilaration of diagnosis. Everyone there was a relative or friend. As I introduced myself, they moved from their chairs to a standing semicircle, close before me. Someone said, "Let Momma up front," and a short, heavy woman with gray-streaked hair and a melancholy, weary look tentatively stepped forward.

"Mr. Johnson is awake, but cannot move," I said. They hung on my every inflection. My body and voice became stony, so the relatives could concentrate on my words and so I might control my own response to this tragedy if their emotions broke free. My face took on an impassive expression that felt like something I had seen in my father when he gathered in his emotions. We revert to our most primitive imprints under stress sometimes.

"You mean he's had a stroke?" gasped an elderly woman who fingered rosary beads.

"Yes," I replied, relieved they seemed prepared for this disaster. "It's a rare and serious stroke that has damaged the bottom half of a part of his brain called the pons. It's a bridge that carries messages for movement between the spinal cord and the cerebral hemispheres."

"I thought you got paralyzed on one side with a stroke," asserted a young man wearing black-framed glasses.

A woman to my right said scoldingly, "Bobby, let the doctor talk."

"I'm afraid in this case the lack of blood flow occurred in the brain stem, a small area, but vitally important for movement. Doctors would say he's 'locked-in,' meaning his body is paralyzed, but his mind works okay. He cannot speak or move, but he can blink his eyes, once to answer yes, and twice for no."

Bobby broke in again. "The doctor downstairs in Emergency, Dr. Frankfort, said the CAT scan was normal. So what are you saying about a stroke?"

"It's either too early to see the stroke or the lesion's too small to show up. The CT helps us know that there's no bleeding, but a serious stroke best explains what I found."

"Lord, Lord have mercy," a woman cried out.

47

I hoped so. The repugnant thought of living as a brain attached to tubes for all needs was mollified by my knowledge that he would either improve greatly or die soon. I told them we would do everything possible, but offered no prognosis since no one asked.

I checked Oubre at seven-thirty that morning; he looked less disheveled and spoke in a stronger whisper. I had planned to reassess Gallagher and Johnson at noon, but my last morning office consultation with Mr. Harvey Block took me through the lunch hour.

Block, a retired adult-movie projectionist, complained that his fingers and toes wiggled. After examining him, it appeared to me that he was wiggling them on purpose.

"I'm not. They wiggle by themselves." He tweaked his thumbs against his middle fingers as if snapping them, while simultaneously rubbing each of his big toes over its neighbor.

"It looks like you're in control. Maybe you're wiggling them because they feel odd," I offered.

"Well, I can stop 'em, but they want to go on wiggling." His digits rested. "See, I just stopped 'em, against their will. The wife can stop 'em, too."

"The wife can stop the wiggling?" I mimicked.

"Yeah. She yells at me and them and they stop. See, I like settin' barefooted on the couch and they catch her eye watching TV. Boy, does she get pissed. One day we was driving to Las Vegas . . ."

I interrupted. "Mr. Block, let me ask you something again. Do your fingers or toes feel numb or tingle or burn?"

"Hard to say. Did I tell you about the crappins in my neck? Orthoplegic surgeon says I got 'em." He dropped his head back and rolled it side to side. "Hear the crappins?"

Waylaid again, I corrected, "You mean crepitance, grinding sounds from creaking joints. Everyone has that to some degree, but it doesn't necessarily mean anything's wrong. What about the tingling in your hands and feet?"

"Wouldn't put it that way, but yeah, they are kinda numb."

"You said you don't drink alcohol?" I asked again, as I had before my exam.

"No, haven't touched the stuff."

"Never?" I pursued.

"Maybe socially." He hunched forward, as if leaning over a cocktail glass at a bar. His tongue lashed at the corners of his mouth.

"How often's that?"

"Oh, you know, with the wife or boys I bowl with. Now there's a fellow from my Hollywood High class, always talked in history class and got an A. I never spoke and got a C. Never was the loquacious sort. He just reminded me of that when he got that award from the P.T.A."

"Mr. Block," I broke in, "why are you telling me this?"

"Well, like I was saying, now this fellow could drink." Harvey's fingers, toes, and tongue darted furiously. I fisted my fingers to prevent them from snapping sympathetically.

"What would you drink with him?"

"Oh, a coupla beers."

"Did you ever have more than a few?"

"Sometimes I might take in a six-pack or two in an evening." His small brown eyes squinted, inspecting the rose and green mermaid tattooed on his right forearm.

"How many evenings a week would you do that?" I continued.

"Not more than a few." He nodded his head innocently and his eyelids closed in a restful way.

"Would you drink something else other nights?"

"Well, I wouldn't drink beer with the wife. She likes a mixed drink and I'm partial to vodka."

My verbal scalpel was about to cut into the truth. "How many vodkas do you have a night?"

"Might a had a few. Like mine in a tall glass without a lotta ice."

"Anything else?"

"Sometimes we'll have a magnum of wine."

"How many bottles of vodka do you buy each week?"

"I'd pick up several sometimes. I'm not trying to keep anything from you, Doc."

"Mr. Block. Do you ever feel shaky if you don't have a drink?"

"I used to wake up kinda trembling, but it went away with a vodka and juice."

"When was that?" I rubbed my nose, hiding a yawn. My night with Johnson was catching up and I was hungry for lunch.

"Haven't had that in, say, two to three months. Wasn't eating right and one of the broads where I bowl said I was getting fat. So I cut back on my cocktails." He squinted at me and his tongue curled out like a lizard snatching a fly. "You look tired. Great to be young and making money. Bet you have yourself a time. But I get my six hours these days. No running around. Though you gotta admit I look pretty good for a man of seventy."

"So do you drink now?" I asked again.

"Right. I don't drink. Just a glass of wine with dinner."

Harvey Block was an alcoholic. His peripheral nerves, those traveling to the hands and feet, had been damaged from drinking and poor nutrition, and the resulting numbness made them uncomfortable. He responded by shaking them out. Gallagher had similar dysesthesias from his Guillain-Barré syndrome, a disease that had to cure itself. Harvey could stop drinking to control what he inflicted on himself. I started him on vitamins to assist the healing process, an anticonvulsant drug that might lessen the signals his damaged nerves sent into his brain, and asked him to consider some counseling about his alcohol abuse if he could not stop on his own.

As Harvey walked out, he said, "Doc, don't worry about me. I can stop from having a drink any time. If you say the time's now, I'll do it. But you oughta get yourself a beer. It'll stop that gurgling in your belly."

* * *

By late that afternoon, Moses Johnson no longer blinked his lids, and his pupils were dilated and did not narrow to light. His heart pumped, though his blood pressure sometimes dropped so low that his internist had to push intravenous medications to raise it. Clear urine flowed into a plastic bag at bedside and the respirator breathed for him. But he showed no nervous-system function.

I called in our electroencephalography technician, who promptly pasted twenty-one electrode wires to Johnson's scalp and recorded his brain's waves. In a normal, awake person, we'd expect to see the machine's pens trace about eight to twelve rhythmical, smooth peaks and valleys each second. This so-called alpha rhythm reflects the cumulative electrical activity of neurons in the cortex, which are excited and inhibited by deeper neurons in the brain stem and thalamus. With damage to the brain, this rhythm slows and becomes irregular over the site of injury. On Johnson's EEG, the pens drew only straight lines. Nothing fired the cortex. The stroke had extended another inch or two into his brain stem's gray and white substance (the same area threatened by Oubre's cerebral swelling), necrotizing what remained of Johnson's vital activating centers. His brain was dead.

As I watched Johnson's heart pulse against his chest wall, a tension headache began to throb reflexively in my neck and temples. I am still a reluctant expert in the determination of brain death and in stopping support. Becoming the primary-care physician for the mechanically preserved who have little or no cerebral function is one of those negative fringe benefits you never know about until you're already a trained specialist.

In the waiting room, where the Johnson clan continued their vigil, I explained Moses's deterioration. If, in twenty-four hours, he showed no neurologic function by my exam and no cerebral electrical activity by EEG, we could be certain, beyond any medical doubt, that his brain would never function again. If another physician agreed, California law permitted us to stop all drug and mechanical supports. The women sobbed openly, but Johnson's powerfully built nephew glared at me.

"You mean with Mrs. Johnson's say-so you doctors can take the man off the respirator." The group seemed to edge a half step toward me.

I directly confronted him. "Dr. Frankfort and I want you to feel comfortable with what has happened. If you want to bring other family in to see him, we can hold off a short time. But this isn't a situation where the family has to make a decision about turning off the respirator. The law frees you of that responsibility."

"Look," he said, "you know what happened to those Kaiser doctors. You better be sure everything's cool. We want everything possible done for my uncle."

He referred to a surgeon and internist at Kaiser Permanente, the largest HMO in the country, who had been arraigned for allegedly murdering a patient. In 1981, this man in his sixties suffered a cardiac arrest and severe brain damage at the end of a minor surgical procedure. Three days later, his doctors told the wife he would never recover, so she consented to disconnect him from the respirator. Apparently much to their surprise, the patient continued breathing on his own, just as in the court-ordered withdrawal of mechanical support from Karen Ann Quinlan. So the doctors, believing they acted out of compassion, denied him food and fluids for a week, until he died. A Los Angeles district attorney claimed the doctors stepped beyond what the law permits and premeditatedly killed him. The court cleared the physicians of any wrongdoing before the case could go to trial.

"The Kaiser affair was different," I said, noticing that the family was becoming confused. "When someone's brain is so seriously damaged from a cardiac arrest or trauma, or occasionally a stroke, that he'll never be even slightly independent again, the spouse and children may consider whether or not to continue extraordinary measures that prolong the victim's life. In that case, it's not a doctor's arbitrary decision and there's no way for the law or science or any moral code to dictate what is best done. In Mr. Johnson's case, his brain has been destroyed by the stroke, much more than irreparably damaged. His brain is dead, so he is dead. You must understand that brain death is as real a death as if the heart stopped beating. The actual moment of death sometimes gets lost in all our medical technology."

The nephew looked at Johnson's daughter and said, "Maybe we should get a lawyer checking this out."

"That's okay if you wish, but please consider that prolonging this support can become a sort of mutilation to his body and your memory of him. We have to face up to the end."

The wife, two children, and a teenaged niece asked to see Johnson. The others sat motionless, staring at their hands and feet. At bedside, the niece began crying and begged me not to let her uncle die. His eyes were still open, she pointed out, so maybe he could see. And his chest expanded as the respirator pumped, so where there was movement, there was life. I looked to Mrs. Johnson for help. She sighed and massaged her husband's hand below the taped intravenous needle in his forearm. Her eyes wandered up the translucent tubing to hanging bottles of saline and dopamine wrapped in crinkled aluminum foil. She briefly studied the rest of his support—the respirator's bellows, the central venous pressure line under his clavicle, the squiggles of monitors, the businesslike nurses.

She said to the niece and her adult children, "He's not with us anymore. I know what the doctor's saying." And to me she added, "We all understand and thank you." They each touched his face and left in tears.

The next morning, I stood by Moses Johnson and watched his EEG. The blue lines were straight and parallel; no brain activity. But I found myself reviewing the details of his case to feel certain he was dead.

No one in the family wanted to be present. That made it easier to break my bond with the patient. I disconnected his endotracheal tube from a coil of plastic tubing wet with droplets of the respirator's humidified air. As I watched to see if he would breathe on his own, my mind numbed into something like a light sleep, a protective withdrawal that still could not prevent a tension headache from slowly arising in my neck and temples. The familiar sounds of his monitoring devices, tones usually linked to a patient's well-being, became hypnotic.

Suddenly, an alarm like a continuously ringing telephone startled me. For a moment, I couldn't locate its source. Then I realized it was from the respirator, a safety feature warning of an accidental disconnection. My hand ran over the twenty dials almost blindly, until I found the "off" switch and flipped it hard. The soft beeps and green blips of heart and blood-pressure tracings faded in five minutes.

FOUR

THE TWINS SQUEALED WITH PLEASURE Sunday afternoon as Barbara and I skimmed them across the surface of the pool. The ginger and coconut scent of late-blooming white gardenias competed with the smell of the smoke rising from the hamburgers I was charcoal broiling. And then, the lovely Laura May rang.

"Dr. Dobkin," she said, "I know you aren't on call this weekend, but Dr. Charles insists on speaking to you. Says it's urgent."

"Put him on." I couldn't imagine why an anesthesiologist would want me.

"Bruce, something terrible's happened to Sandy Waterford's wife. She's in a hyperbaric chamber on Catalina Island, convulsing. Sandy's there and wanted me to see if you could help out."

Ira knew few details. Sandy, a dermatologist with whom I often chatted in the doctors' dining room, took his wife, Cynthia, scuba diving with some friends who owned a motorboat. On the last dive of the day, he suddenly realized that Cynthia had left his side. After searching along a ridge of rocks at a depth of thirty-five to forty feet, he surfaced. In the distance, he could see his friends lift Cynthia into the anchored boat. She was unconscious and pulseless by the time they had noticed her bobbing on a kelp bed fifty yards away. Sandy estimated that no more than six minutes has passed from the last moment he saw her to the time they pulled her on deck.

They immediately began mouth-to-mouth resuscitation and chest compression. The boat headed toward Catalina Island, and their frantic effort paid off: They had managed to manually squeeze enough blood and oxygen through Cynthia's circulation to revive her heart's electrical system. Then, as blood filled her brain stem's respiratory center, she began to take short gasps on her own. But she didn't show a sign of waking up. When they reached a Coast Guard medical station on the rustic island twenty minutes later, Cynthia's breathing and heartbeat had stopped again. Sandy and his friends restarted CPR while the doctor on duty slipped an intravenous line into the crook of her elbow and shot in a series of drugs that might stimulate her heart. When that failed, he jolted her with all four hundred watts from a defibrillator. Finally, her heart's muscle pumped. Then they put her into a hyperbaric chamber.

The doctor on duty, a medical resident at Los Angeles County Hospital, could not be sure whether her heart stopped because water had filled Cynthia's lungs or because air collapsed them. If a diver ascends too fast without exhaling, air in the lungs reaches a higher pressure than the surrounding pressure. Delicate pockets in the lung tissue called alveoli, which ordinarily exchange oxygen with blood capillaries, overinflate until some blow out. Air then escapes inside the chest and acts like a balloon that inflates and compresses the heart or lungs beyond their ability to function. Even worse, bubbles of air may break into the bloodstream like microscopic balloons called emboli and clog blood flow to all organs, especially the brain. Treatment in the chamber would repressurize her, creating the same conditions as if she were under eighty feet of water. In this way, any air bubbles that plugged her blood vessels would be forced to shrink and dissipate. Slow depressurization back to normal atmospheric pressure would then rid the body of these emboli—but not necessarily before they had robbed Cynthia's brain cells of blood flow and damaged them beyond repair.

The resident at Catalina did what he could, without equipment for blood tests or x-rays, to prevent Cynthia's heart and lungs from giving up again. But it was her brain that most worried him. As the motor neurons of Cynthia's cortex fired volleys of seizure discharges, they conducted every muscle of her face, trunk, and limbs to jerk in synchronous spasms. Her cortical neurons must have been seriously injured by the loss of blood flow and oxygen during her cardiac arrests. While her convulsions continued, she could not breath adequately and the fierce muscle contractions allowed toxic acids to build up in the blood.

The brain's cortex, or gray matter, contains about ten billion nerve cells that are linked to one another via hundreds of thousands of miles of bushy connections called dendrites. These extension cords receive incoming electrical and chemical messages at specialized points of contact called synapses. Each nerve-cell body also sprouts a long, thin cable called an axon, which can reach a yard or more from the brain's surface down through the brain stem and the spinal cord. These axons, each wrapped in a fatty white coat called myelin, form the brain's white matter. Every neuron is potentially a highly charged battery. Over a million chemical pumps in each cell's membrane maintain this charge. Under ordinary circumstances, there's a constant influx of signals from surrounding dendrites to excite and inhibit the cell. When the brain receives a tremendous injury like Cynthia's, the exciting signals take over and convulsions result. Anticonvulsant drugs help cool down this electrochemical excitement in the membrane and enhance the effects of the inhibitory network of bushy dendrites around it.

Over the static of the radio-telephone, I asked the resident at Catalina to inject a large dose of an anticonvulsant he had not yet tried in order to attempt to control Cynthia's seizures. He returned to the line a few minutes later and reported that the drug had stopped them. He'd arrange for helicopter transport to Freeman as soon as she could safely leave the hyperbaric chamber.

I told Barbara what had happened. "She's going to be brain damaged, isn't she?"

"A prolonged cardiac arrest, seizures, maybe air emboli to the brain," I answered cautiously. "It's got to be bad."

The phone rang again. "Yes, Laura May."

"It's your mother, son."

"What's wrong?"

"It's your father. The headaches are back and this morning he fell against the piano. I mean, I can't clear all the rugs and furniture out of the house. You can't live like that." She burst into tears. "It's gotten so that I can't even remember what he was like when he was well."

"I know. Maybe he should come here again. It'll give you a break."

"You talk to him. He doesn't listen to me."

After a few moments, my father picked up the phone in his bedroom and asked, "How are my babies?"

"Your granddaughters are great. You should have seen them in the pool this afternoon. In fact, it's time to pay us a visit. How about coming out later in the week?"

"The balance isn't too good. I don't think I could make the trip."

"Did you get hurt today?"

"The usual. I had a good day on Friday, but I'm just no good."

"Come out and I'll arrange some special therapies at Freeman."

"I don't know. Your mother needs me here. I'm going to lay down." His phone clicked off.

58

My mother said, "What am I going to do? He said he'd do anything for some relief, so the surgeon's talking about trying an operation. But it's his mind. What is *wrong* with him?"

"We've been through that too many times. Get him a plane ticket. Look, how about if I call you tomorrow? I've got to make some arrangements for a patient." I paused a moment. "Remember when I was playing stickball in the alley and some kid pushed that cast-iron clothesline pole over and cracked my skull?"

"How could anyone forget that? You lost so much blood."

"Didn't dad carry me to his car and drive me to a hospital? For some reason, I remember sirens and being wheeled on a gurney."

"Your father saw the ambulance coming after we drove a few blocks from the house and he swerved the car in front of it. He must've thought he was back in a Jeep. I went with you in the ambulance and he followed. What made you think of that?"

"Something I saw, I guess. He was a different person back then. I'll talk to you. Don't forget the plane ticket."

I got on the phone again and put together a team of doctors in preparation for Cynthia's arrival: an internist to quarterback, pulmonary and heart specialists, and a thoracic surgeon. None of them were on call that Sunday, but they responded like good neighbors in a crisis. At ten, Sandy telephoned in an unwavering voice. "We're leaving the island and should be at Freeman in forty-five minutes. Cynthia's gonna be okay. Please do everything you can." We would.

The crew waited in the intensive care unit. We pieced together all the information we had gained from several more calls to the medical station and shared what we understood about the complications of drowning, barotrauma, and air emboli. Portable x-ray equipment, a respirator, surgical instruments, IV solutions, and an assortment of tubes encased in clear plastic trays stood ready. We wanted to construct a safety net around Cynthia that would allow nothing else to go wrong.

The internist and an emergency-room doctor and nurse met the helicopter at a lighted landing pad a few steps away from the E.R. Sandy had been squeezing a black breathing bag connected to her endotracheal tube to deepen her respiration. They hooked her up to a respirator, the nurse drew a half-dozen tubes of blood, and they wheeled her into the ICU.

The team quickly surrounded Cynthia and went to work. Her blood pressure was dangerously low. The cardiologist slipped thin catheters into an artery at her wrist and into the large veins that emptied into her heart, so we could monitor the oxygen and fluid pressures of Cynthia's heart and lungs. He studied the first EKG tracings while the surgeon punched a half-inch-wide tube through her right chest wall to expand the lung that an x-ray had shown to have been collapsed by the air that had escaped into her chest. That brought her blood pressure up to normal. Nurses pulled a sheet between her legs and partly over her chest, then passed a soft rubber catheter into her bladder to keep it empty. Stethoscope in ears, the pulmonary specialist listened to her lungs, interpreted the latest chest x-rays, and adjusted her respirator's dials whenever a new set of blood-gas measurements came back from the lab. Time became as meaningless as it is for compulsive gamblers in a casino. We updated one another with numbers and conjectures, pushed medications, and spoke in somber voices.

Everyone wanted my prognosis as soon as possible. I foraged in and out among the team and the plastic tubing that formed a stringy curtain about the bed. If Cynthia were not salvageable now and her heart arrested again, we might hesitate going all-out in yet another resuscitation effort.

Cynthia lay quietly with her eyes half-open. She was one of those shapely, unmuscled women who stay trim more by diet than exercise. Her body was tan, her nose and shoulders pink from the day's outing. It seemed as if she should awaken any moment after a rest from her day at the beach. But even the pain of needles plunged into her arms and chest did not arouse her. Her eyes didn't move, her pupils were widely dilated and would not constrict to my pen light, and she did not gag when I touched the back of her throat with a cotton swab. Her tendon reflexes jerked briskly, and when I scraped the bottom of each foot, her big toes curled involuntarily upward in a so-called Babinski sign. These uninhibited primitive reflexes were a sign that the long motor pathway from Cynthia's cortex to spinal cord had been damaged. When I pressed my finger against her brow, her arms flexed up against her chest, her hands made a fist, and her legs jerked straight, then relaxed; this reflex, so-called decorticate rigidity, pointed to a severe injury to the pathways between thalamus and cortex.

Cynthia was in a deep coma; unresponsive and unconscious, her will, comprehension, emotions, and awareness of any internal or external stimulus were unarousable. This meant she suffered a disconnection between the reticular activating system's furnace in the brain stem and the cortex that, via the thalamus, electrifies it into wakefulness. Most likely, the cortical neurons of both hemispheres could not receive or handle any useful transmissions, because lack of oxygen and blood had damaged or destroyed most of them.

After an hour of intensive manipulations and then cautious fine tuning, the team retreated a few yards from the foot of Cynthia's bed. A nurse unraveled Cynthia's bed sheet and covered her, hiding the signs of our intrusion. The wall behind her had become a collage of colored bottles, brushed metal, and intertwined tubes and cords. Sandy moved to her side and folded his arms on top of the bed rail. The air was humid and subdued. Other patients were too ill or drowsy to notice us. I leaned against the counter at the nurses' station, watched the gray respirator's bellows rise and fall, and listened to the bubbling from the suction tube, which took the air that had been compressing her right lung and emptied it into a container of water.

The internist began, "There's not much more to do. By tomorrow, she'll probably develop pulmonary complications from the saltwater drowning."

"Yeah, she's incredibly stable," said the cardiologist absentmindedly. He turned to me. "What do you think?"

I hesitated, especially with Sandy so close, and turned my back to him. "Her age is in her favor," I said, "although even under the best circumstances, fewer than half the people who suffer a cardiac arrest wake up, and many of those who do are not very functional. From what Sandy told me, her brain probably got no blood or oxygen for at least ten minutes." I did not have to spell out what that meant.

Within only five minutes, a brain deprived of blood flow starts to soften into a creamy liquid, and the machinery that makes the neurons run begins to disintegrate. Even with CPR, the brain gets under half the amount of blood flow it ordinarily needs.

"And with a lung collapsed, who knows how much oxygen she got into her brain? What's worse, I suspect we're also dealing with air emboli to the brain that could have plugged a lot of cerebral vessels before they got her into the hyperbaric chamber. That can only magnify the extent of neuronal destruction."

"You think she'll be a vegetable?" asked the pulmonary specialist with his index finger on his nose and hand cupped over his mouth.

"I don't think there's much hope, but we ought to err on the side of going all-out. We'll know the prognosis for certain within the next few days. If she does not show us at least some semipurposeful limb and eye movements over the next forty-eight hours, at least a sign that her nervous system can function, the chances she'll walk or ever take care of herself are very dim."

As we stood there frozen by the tragedy within our own clan, I recalled the trouble I had gotten into six years ago on a dive for lobsters off the Los Angeles coast. After forty minutes in cold, turbulent water, my partner signaled that he was low on air, so he kicked toward the surface. I casually followed. Thin stalks of kelp attached to the sea floor grew sparsely at that depth. About five feet from the surface, the other diver became entangled in the slimy, knobby seaweed of branching kelp leaves. He panicked and lost his mask and air hose. I pulled out my knife and hacked the mesh away from him. I tried to give him air from my tank and release his weight belt so he would float to the surface, but his thrashing dislodged my mask and mouthpiece. A thousand octopus arms of kelp enveloped me. Repeatedly, I reached to release my weight belt and find my air-tank hose, but pulled in only kelp. I struggled to the surface, inhaled a half breath of air through my snorkel, then choked on briny water as the lead weights around my waist pulled me under again. My nervous system exploded into a desperate surge against water, kelp, lead, gagging nausea, and near suffocation. Suddenly, something encircled my bursting chest. I started to fight it off, then forced myself to relax when I realized that it was an arm. A diver from our boat dragged me onto a lifesaver. My partner, retching and quivering, also clung to one. Before this moment in the ICU, I had never considered how vulnerable I was.

Suddenly, Cynthia arched her back and thrust her arms and legs in a stiff extension. Sandy looked at me with raised eyebrows. I moved toward him with reluctance.

"It's a reflex, Sandy, not really a good sign." But he refused to accept my diagnosis.

"At least she's moving. Right now, I don't care why. I'm just glad there were experienced people on the boat who knew CPR. And the guys at the hyperbaric chamber were great." In the same breath, out of context, like some barely suppressed, racing thought, he asked, "Will you get a CT scan to check out Cynthia's brain?"

"In the morning. It's already after midnight. Besides, a CT probably won't show us what's going on. Cynthia's injury at this point is at a biochemical level. It's inside the nerve cells."

We are just beginning to understand why neurons die after a brief spell of anoxia and no blood flow. Many other cells of the body tolerate such insults. There are even some neurons that can withstand a lack of blood perfusion for longer periods than others. It seems that the most vulnerable neurons are the ones that quickly deplete their energy stores and then alter their metabolism to convert whatever glucose is available into enough energy to stay alive. All they end up doing is producing a by-product, lactic acid, that damages the cell even more. But the biggest problem for a slightly ravaged nerve cell after a few minutes of cardiac standstill is what happens when CPR restores some blood flow. A massive amount of calcium, always present in and around cells, suddenly flows into the neuron and damages the cell's membranes. This releases chemicals that then attack and destroy the rest of the neuron. In a sense, the neurons mistakenly cannibalize themselves.

"We'd see if there's any edema or a stroke on CT, wouldn't we?" Sandy asked.

"It might show up, if that's part of her problem. But that wouldn't change what we're doing. The electroencephalogram will tell us more about her susceptibility to seizures and give us a baseline of her brain's function."

The electrical discharges that cause muscles to jerk rhythmically during a seizure show up on the EEG as a pointed squiggle, called a sharp or spike, instead of a rounded one. And, in a general way, the slower the EEG rhythm, the greater the injury we can infer to cortical neurons. I hesitated uncomfortably, then asked, "How do you feel?"

"I'm okay. At first, I thought I lost her." He clasped both hands around her left one and rotated her gold wedding band. "At least she's alive. I have something. I guess for a few hours I thought it was all over."

"Do the kids know?"

"No. The girls are at a camp back east. Same camp Cynthia went to when she was their age."

"Everything's stable now. Maybe you should get some sleep."

"Should I call her folks in Miami?" he asked, as if I knew what people must do in a tragedy.

"It's awfully late."

"Yeah. You know, she's scared of scuba diving." He sighed and squeezed her hand. "I guess I wanted her to overcome that fear."

FIVE

OUBRE'S EYES STAYED SHUT when I greeted him Monday morning and opened for only a moment as I jostled him. In a fraction of that stuporous moment, I thought he recognized me. But a dead-animal smell, the odor of bacterial decay, emerged from his mouth.

His pattern of breathing had changed since I examined him Friday. For about thirty seconds, he would take increasingly deep and rapid breaths in a smooth build-up, reach a peak and wane in an equally smooth decrescendo. Then he would stop breathing for about twenty seconds until his lips turned blue and the cycle restarted.

Normally, the rate and depth of breathing is regulated by the amount of carbon dioxide present from moment to moment in the blood. Brain-stem centers measure this and automatically tell the muscles that expand the chest how hard to work. Oubre's pattern, so-called Cheyne-Stokes respirations, indicated that his brain stem's sensitivity to carbon dioxide had diminished. He would stop breathing until the gas built up to a very high level, then hyperventilate long past the time its level had fallen. Oubre's intracranial pressure must have risen dangerously again, upsetting his brain stem's vital centers.

I called the intern on a hospital phone. "What did you think of Oubre today?"

"Seems more or less stable since yesterday," he offered.

"What about the eye signs? Did you check them?"

"Ah, well, they seemed okay."

"I believe he's about to herniate again. We have to treat more aggressively. I'll wait for you."

A few minutes later, a chatty, white-coated entourage of two interns, a senior resident I once trained in neurology for a month, their faculty attending physician, and two students joined me at Oubre's bedside. They looked like a high-school senior class on a trip to the local hospital. I reproduced my examination for them.

Oubre's intern nervously scratched above his ear and watched with knitted brows. The other house staff and their students shifted their weight from leg to leg, hands behind their backs, and spared the intern the usual look of indictment. The young man had made the worst kind of error: He either missed the key signs or did not check for them. If nothing else, a doctor must train himself to be compulsive in his evaluation and honest about his findings.

The intern blinked his pen light into Oubre's pupils with the to-and-fro swing of a pathfinder's lantern and concluded, "Essentially, I think there's been a significant worsening."

"It's extraordinary, isn't it?" I injected quickly. "He's on the verge of herniation again." My own clinical teachers had once spared me for real and imagined mistakes.

When I was a fourth-year medical student at Temple University, my last rotation in the hospital before graduation placed me on an old medical ward, with the responsibilities of an intern. The ward had originally been built as a ten-room annex to isolate patients with infectious diseases like tuberculosis. By the time I worked there, it housed the sickest people

I've ever seen. Everyone had at least two organs failing. One patient, a diminutive black man named Tony, was a living laboratory for the practice of acute medicine.

We admitted Tony at the start of my rotation. He was forty-two and looked sixty, because he suffered with congestive heart failure, liver failure, pancreatitis, a profound anemia, a fever from pneumonia, and was so badly swollen from his nipples to his toes that I could sink my finger into the spongy skin of his chest or thigh until only the last knuckle showed. A pinprick to his leg produced a few drops of water instead of blood. But he vomited plenty of blood.

Tony was dying from alcoholism and malnutrition. For a month, I filled him full of antibiotics, protein, and red cells, and titrated a pharmacy of drugs for every organ. Although I sometimes thought I was over my head in figuring out how to manage his case, I began to feel, when Tony finally improved, that medical school really had transformed me into a potentially competent doctor. And we grew chummy, talking about the Phillies, his career playing piano in small bars, the time he spent working as a pimp, and his alcoholism. No one aside from me visited him.

Four days before my graduation, I treated Tony and his nurse to cheese-steak sandwiches and pizza. He had lost forty-five pounds of edema fluid and was doing well enough to be discharged when I left the ward. I was on call that evening and slept on a cot at the back of the ward. Late into the night, I became aware that a nurse was shaking me. "Doctor, Doctor, please," she whispered, "you must see this man!" She handed me a patient's chart and I followed her, half-asleep, down the darkened corridor to a patient who had become acutely short of breath. When I finished treating him, I looked across the room and saw Tony lying motionless in his bed, his right arm and leg hanging loosely over the side of the mattress.

"Tony," I called and jostled his shoulder. I grabbed his chin, opened his eyelids, and then realized what had happened. "Tony," I said. "You were going home."

I listened for breath and heart sounds, but all I heard was the amplified rasp of the stethoscope's head settling on his cool skin. The nurse handed me his bulky chart. I wrote:

> Patient well known to me was found without spontaneous respirations or pulse. No brain-stem function evident. Roommate offered that patient made "a funny little gagging noise" an hour ago, then didn't move anymore. No resuscitation attempted. Cause of death—cardiac arrest from cardiomyopathy and arrhythmia or pulmonary embolus. Time of death—3:05 A.M.

An autopsy revealed that a blood clot came loose from a vein in his leg and blocked the flow of blood to his lungs. The resident said we were lucky Tony had improved at all. Death, he said, is not a doctor's failure.

I led the U.C.L.A. entourage to the end of the ICU and said, "Dr. Oubre's condition can change fast. We'll have to monitor him with great care and make some immediate changes in our treatment."

The house staff listened carefully as I explained what we knew about the evolution of a cerebral infarction and edema. When blood flow ceases, the membrane and inner machinery of the neurons in the cerebral hemispheres fail and salts and water rush into the crippled cells. The involved brain turns soft and pale. More water leaks into the tissue around the cells and the brain grows boggier and boggier. Within a week or so, the water stops accumulating, the neurons and their axons disintegrate, and blood pigment from trapped red corpuscles turns the injured area yellow. Scavenger cells, glittering with digestive enzymes, eat much of what remains. After a month, a milky cyst evolves. Oubre's stroke was nearly ten days old. The fluid in his brain should stop collecting soon, if we could hold off the threat of herniation one last time. I wondered what would be left of Larry's mind, should he survive, but I said nothing that might detract from the group's effort. We decided to put Oubre on a respirator again, give him more anti-edema drugs, and cut back sharply on his fluid intake. And we hoped he was strong enough to get through this crisis.

I was over a half-hour late for the office, so I had to put off seeing Cynthia Waterford and Dick Gallagher until noon. A Middle Eastern businessman in his fifties was first on the morning's agenda.

"Ah, you're here," he berated. "I'm a punctual man with important matters to take care of."

"Sorry, but I had a sick patient. How are you doing?"

"I have no further problems with the headaches. I must say, I considered not even paying you for what seemed like silly advice, but the injection and all has worked."

He had complained of daily headaches, "like the Ayatollah's guards are tightening a belt around my skull." He denied any association of pain with stress. The dull, steady headaches most often occurred hours after doing chin-ups at home and as he drove on the freeway. When I first examined him a month ago, the only abnormal finding was marked tenderness over several palpable knots in the muscles at the back of his right shoulder and neck. I numbed the painful trigger points with a local anesthetic and a steroid, suggested some stretching exercises for the neck and shoulders, prescribed a nighttime muscle relaxant for a week, and told him to drive his car with his chin tucked in a relaxed military posture. I felt certain he suffered with muscle-contraction headaches, especially since, even in the office, he tensed his neck muscles and jammed the back of his head into his shoulders. He probably spasmed the muscles when he drove his car in heavy, irritating traffic (his annoyance with me confirmed that he could not tolerate waiting) and when he contracted them suddenly doing pull-ups. The exam today revealed much less tenderness and no knots.

"So," he said, smiling, "I don't have a brain tumor or something like that?"

"No, just muscle-contraction headaches. And they'll return if

69

you don't stop carrying so much tension in your neck. For now, I see no reason to do any tests. Call if you need me."

This small victory carried me through the next few cases until Mrs. Browne called. Her husband's chart was brought in by my secretary. I often can't remember who the patient is until I read my notes. In this case, I had not seen him in two years.

"Dr. Dobkin?" asked a frustrated, elderly woman. "Pete's getting so much worse that I had to talk to someone. Remember us?"

"Yes," I said, scanning the pages in his chart. "Is the senility getting worse?" Her husband had mild Alzheimer's disease, which by now might be expected to progress.

"Oh, I don't know. He's running around the house filling plastic bags with whatever he can find and says he's going home. I've had to dead-bolt the doors so he can't get out and wander and get lost. He wants to go home and here he is living in the house he built himself twenty-five years ago. He is home. And then, he's up all night drinking soda, then he'll shower at two in the morning. Who can go on like this? Our family doctor says to put him in a home, but I can't do that to Pete."

"Bring him in and I'll take a look."

"Oh, I can't do that. I don't drive and I can't always get someone to take us. I'm afraid to let him out of the house. He seems so agitated."

"Does he sleep at all?"

"Maybe a few hours a day. It's been going on for weeks."

"I'll write a prescription for a nighttime sedative. If he rests properly, he may be less confused."

"What are the side effects?" she asked in a calmer, rather suspicious tone.

"Of the drug? Well, some people with Alzheimer's become lethargic or more confused if we don't hit on the ideal dose right away."

"Well, I can't do that."

"We're only trying the drug for its potential benefit."

"It sounds too risky."

Losing patience, I suggested, "Check it out with your doctor. I really shouldn't prescribe for someone I haven't seen in two years."

"Nobody wants to help . . ."

"Mrs. Browne. You're making a difficult problem worse for yourself. Did you ever join one of the Alzheimer's support groups?"

"No. But . . ."

"When you talk to your family doctor, ask him about that too. Or my secretary can give you their number. I'd be happy to see Mr. Browne any time you can get him here."

My next consultation greeted me in the sugary, precise vocal melody of a tape-recorded message from the telephone company's directory assistance. She wore the putty-colored slacks of a security guard and sported long pink fingernails, each punctuated with a tiny red rhinestone.

While patrolling a high-rise construction site, she had been knocked to the ground by a small van backing out of a driveway. She broke the fall with her right hand and bruised her left thigh. By the next day, she felt pins and needles in the front of the thigh and occasional numbness in her right hand, and both shoulders ached. Her physician suspected a pinched nerve in her neck or back. My history and exam suggested two other diagnoses.

The tingling in her left thigh resulted from a bruise or stretch of her lateral femoral cutaneous nerve, a hair-thin branch that transmits the sensations of touch, sharpness, and temperature from the skin of the thigh to the spinal cord. Her right hand's numbness, which bothered her usually when driving, heralded a carpal-tunnel syndrome. A peripheral nerve, called the median nerve, crosses the middle of each wrist via a canal walled in by bone, tendons, and tough connective tissue. Any prolonged bending of the wrist, while writing, for instance, or when holding a steering wheel or sleeping in an awkward position, stretches and compresses the nerve. The nerve sends a tingling message to the brain that it is being assaulted. I stimulated the median nerve above her wrist with a small electrical jolt and found that the time it took for the impulse to cross her wrist into her hand was mildly delayed. This confirmed my suspicion that her injury had partially blocked the nervous system's own signals.

"Don't worry, you'll be fine. These are common problems with easy solutions," I assured her. "I'll give you a wrist splint to wear at night that will probably prevent any further hand numbness. If it gets worse or if you have pain, numbness, or weakness in the hand, then a rather simple operation can be performed to widen the canal. And if the thigh bothers you, I can give you a medication that will block the nerve's signals of numbness."

"Doctor, I must worry." Her head cocked back and she sat straighter, then froze again with a stringent, condescending smile. "Don't tell me not to worry. What if I go to write a report and my hand feels numb and I must put the pen down? Or what if my leg gives out when I'm alone on night patrol, a woman unable to perform? You see, Doctor, my husband walked out on me after twenty-two years of marriage, and it is not easy for a forty-five year-old person to find a decent vocation. I must be healthy."

"You're in no danger. These are tingles, not paralyzing conditions. But I'll suggest that your employer continue you on disability one more week, until I review how well you're doing."

"Well, I do hope that will be sufficient."

After lunch, I found Sandy in the ICU talking to his wife from behind the head of her bed. His arms cradled her head and his mouth nearly touched her ear. A nurse reported that Dr. Waterford had been whispering like that for an hour. Before anyone examined her or drew blood or shot an x-ray, he requested a moment to introduce the person and tell Cynthia what would happen next.

Sandy greeted me enthusiastically. "I was just telling

Cynthia why she needs a respirator. I know you can't say for sure if she hears me, but maybe she can. I mean, there's a lot of strange stuff going on here, if you've never been in an intensive care unit."

The only sign that Cynthia's nervous system was functioning at all was the occasional abrupt arching of her back accompanied by rigid spasms in her arms and legs. Had I sliced both cerebral hemispheres away from Cynthia's upper brain stem, like cutting a head of broccoli from its stalk, I would still be able to evoke this sort of primitive spasm.

"Not much yet, huh?" Sandy remarked in a deliberate tone. Unshaven, dressed in a wrinkled scrub suit he had worn while trying to sleep on a couch in the surgeons' lounge, he rummaged through his hopes. "Did the EEG show anything?"

"It shows a burst-suppression pattern—irregular, slow electrical activity followed by almost nothing for a few seconds, then another cycle of minimal activity," I answered rather academically. Cynthia's cortical neurons were barely gasping. "The record is typical of a severe anoxic brain injury."

"Well, at least we still have some activity. How about the CT scan?"

"No visible areas of stroke or swelling."

"Great."

"Yeah, some things are in her favor," I offered. "It's amazing that her lungs haven't become waterlogged. Guess she didn't really drown. Most of her trouble stems from the cardiac arrest and the air that burst out of her lungs and into her bloodstream."

I wrote a progress note in her chart: "No change; prognosis for better than a persistent vegetative state is guarded."

Down the corridor, Dick Gallagher remained paralyzed from shoulders to toes with his Guillain-Barré syndrome. But he was stable enough to begin full rehabilitation activities. "Ready to start?"

"Man, I'm overripe. Guess this means you think I won't need a respirator."

"Yeah. You're a rock climber, right?" He nodded, as if he might be climbing tomorrow. "Then you understand that it can be harder to descend after you reach the top then it is to climb up. Your ascent was no picnic. Our therapists can only direct you now. You provide the motivation."

Twenty minutes later, as I waited in the lobby for the elevator to the office my practice rents, my beeper blasted its urgent signal. Almost immediately after this, a young woman turned glum eyes on me and asked, "What floor is room 404 on?" Her boyish companion, who wore a heavy woolen, dark blue, three-piece suit on a warm summer's day, looked apologetically at me but said nothing.

"Suite 404's on the fourth floor, I believe. Turn left when you get off." That was our office; one of my partners had a rather helpless patient on his hands.

"Dr. Dobkin," my secretary scolded as I slipped into my white-cotton coat, "I've been paging you. You got an urgent call for the ICU at U.C.L.A."

Oubre's intern came on the line. Larry was herniating, full scale.

"Dammit," I groaned, "I just don't understand it. We've got to get every spare drop of water out of his brain without knocking down his cerebral blood flow. Give forty . . . no, eighty milligrams of the diuretic and increase the mannitol from the slow drip we started this morning to five hundred milliliters an hour if you have to. Double the dexamethasone. Make sure the carbon dioxide is around twenty-five when you check his blood gases. There's nothing to lose now. If he improves, taper the mannitol very slowly but maintain a constant infusion. And keep checking the sodium, potassium, and BUN. Jesus, just call me as soon as anything changes. If his wife shows up, tell her to call me."

And in walked the young couple who had asked for suite 404.

Carol Barge explained that seven months earlier, she had slipped and landed on her right shoulder. Headaches and neck pain kept her home from her job as a receptionist. Several doctors at her prepaid health plan had treated her symptoms without success, so she and her husband, Tim, were seeking an outside opinion.

"The headaches are horrible," she said without a hint of the body language of pain. "They're killing me. They're constant, worse than migraines. Sometime I think my skull might burst."

"Do you have one now?" I asked.

"Of course. And my right arm aches," she added, running her left hand over the right upper arm, shoulder, and neck. "Sometimes it feels numb, but most times the pain is like daggers of hot metal twisting into me. It's so bad I can't sleep, and then I wake up with a headache. I mean, I've tried Valium and codeine and anything I could get my hands on, and nothing helps these headaches."

"Does anything else bother you?" I asked.

"I get little tingling feelings on the top of my head, and my scalp feels funny when I brush my hair."

"Any other problems?"

Carol served up a virtual smorgasbord of afflictions. Her eyes hurt, her vision momentarily blurred, nothing smelled normal, food tasted metallic, and she endured ringing in her ears. Walking had become unsafe because of dizziness, wooziness, generalized weakness, incoordination, and rubbery legs that threatened to give out. She had become forgetful. Words were lost on the tip of her tongue. And she had lost consciousness a few times, or at least lost track of people's conversations at work when she was under a lot of pressure. Young Mrs. Barge had no appetite, although she had recently gained eight pounds. Her heart skipped beats, she suffered sharp chest pains that took away her breath, and she was losing her hair. Veins bubbled up on the backs of her hands, and blood throbbed in her fingertips. Her skin had turned yellow and dry. Sometimes her urine burned, and diarrhea or constipation dominated her bowel movements for weeks at a time. And two years ago, she noticed some bright blood on the toilet paper with which she wiped herself.

I was about to slip under the general anesthesia of her litany of symptoms. "Do the tips of your fingernails hurt when you urinate?" I broached, biting my cheek so I could continue looking serious.

"I'm not sure," she replied, "but I think I once noticed that." It was impossible to tell if she felt triumphant or worried.

I suspected that Carol Barge simply suffered from a low threshold of pain and a heightened perception of benign aches, tingles, and dizzy-woozies that she could not suppress the way most of us do every day. Hypochondriacs form a legion of the worried well. Of all patients who consult a general practitioner, fifteen to sixty percent suffer with "nonsickness."

The physical exam was no more satisfying than her recital. She stumbled theatrically through the tests of memory and cognition with sluggish, teasingly incomplete answers, then hostile self-correction. When I tested her strength by asking her to resist my hold on her arms and legs, she gave way on her right side with a rachetlike pseudoresistance she insisted was her best. I said, condescendingly, she must try harder. She stopped trying at all.

Testing her cranial nerves was almost entertaining. She blinked and scowled as if soap burned her eyes as she tried to watch my finger move side to side and up and down, and complained that I made her eyeballs hurt. Yet she spontaneously looked off to one side or up at the ceiling without the slightest squint. When I finished peering into the back of her eyes with my ophthalmoscope to check the arteries, veins, and nerve for vision, Mrs. Barge briefly panicked about permanently losing her sight. I explained that light from the instrument, like a flash bulb, causes a brief afterimage. She accepted this as she might a traffic ticket. She was able to stick her tongue out only as far as her lips, despite my exhortations to extend it fully. When I tried to check her gag reflex, her jaws clamped nearly shut.

I attempted an evaluation of her visual fields, a test that requires harmony between patient and doctor. Fixing her vision on my nose as instructed, she appropriately indicated the position of a small red button on a thin wire when it appeared in her peripheral vision. Encouraged, I explored the size of the blind spot in each eye, the small circle just lateral to the center of any point we look at, which marks the location where the optic nerve penetrates the retina. There are no sensory cells on the retina where the optic nerve lies, so there is no vision in that part of the eye.

Ordinarily, the brain deceives us so that we're not aware of this blind spot. The pathways for perception fill in the blank because the brain, through neuronal networks fostered by heredity and experience, tells us there are no holes in the world we perceive. The mind probably plays tricks on our senses as often as our senses fool our minds. That partly explains the richness of our ideas, emotions, and imagination, as well as why three people who observe an automobile accident come up with three different stories about what they saw. And why the brain's grasp of reality falters so easily in the face of disease and psychosis.

Carol Barge's response to my disappearing act wasn't the usual, "Hey, how'd you do that?"

"My God!" she moaned, slapping a hand over her eyes. "I'm losing my vision. I knew something awful was going on." She glared at Tim, who seemed about to protest from the edge of his seat, but sat back in silence.

"Wait, Mrs. Barge," I interrupted. "That's a normal blind spot, something we all have. I was just checking its size and it is fine."

"Please don't keep anything from me."

"I won't. After I finish examining your reflexes and sensation, we'll talk."

I reached for a Queen's Square reflex hammer, a long-handled bludgeon pointed at one end and joined at the other to the center of a round metal disc circumscribed by rubber. It's an unwieldy tool, but it ties me to three centuries of English predecessors the way a stethoscope draped around an internist's neck links him to his medical ancestors.

Carol's knuckles whitened as she grasped the edge of my padded exam table. She flinched each time I gently tapped my hammer over a tendon in her arms. Her left-knee reflex jerked modestly. On the right side, she slammed her foot into my shin. "Must be something wrong with that one," she said innocently.

Mrs. Barge outdid herself in the sensory exam. She could not distinguish a pin's prick from blunt touch over the right side of her face, arm, and leg, but she winced at first when I used the point. She felt the most subtle vibration of my tuning fork against her forehead to the left of her nose, but when I placed a bounding vibration to the right side, she claimed no awareness of its resonant buzz. Barge's response made no physiological sense; vibration carries throughout the skull regardless of where the fork is placed. But it reinforced her belief that the fall damaged her right side.

The examination had only made each of us suspicious about the other's intentions. I said I would check the x-rays already taken and suggested she begin a muscle relaxant and physical therapy to help work out the muscle tenderness in her tense shoulders. Later, I thought to myself, I might inject the most tender spots or trigger points with a local anesthetic and a steroid and possibly start her on an antidepressant drug. But I had to get to know her better before coming at her with a needle or medication with possible side effects.

"The headaches and neck pain should come under control quickly," I reassured her. "They're not indicative of a serious neurologic problem. No pinched nerves or anything to worry about in your brain. As you start to feel better, we can tackle your other symptoms, should they persist."

"Well, I think it's more serious than that. And I've always had medical problems that doctors can't figure out," she stated flatly.

"I thought you mentioned that you hadn't seen any doctors before the accident."

"Not in Los Angeles. Before we moved here, my G.P. in Elmira had me see a thyroid specialist and a cardiologist. You

know, palpitations and weakness. Nothing serious, they said."
She looked down her nose in exasperated disbelief about those
opinions.

"Were you examined by any other physicians or given any
medication?" I asked without enthusiasm.

"Oh, there were others, none any good. They gave me Valium, antidepressants, one thing or another, but always something."

"Have you had any psychological help?"

She paused and sighed. "Yes, I saw a psychiatrist a few
times, if that's what you're getting at. We didn't get along very
well."

"What problems were you having then?" I pressed out of
habit more than interest.

"Oh, I did silly things. My mother insisted I go, but nothing
came of it."

"What things?"

"Just dumb things." She peeked at me as if to make certain I
had not left the room. "Once," she said demurely, "when we
were visiting friends, I guess I took off my pants in their living
room, sat on the floor, and stuffed them under a sofa."

Suddenly, I caught my second wind. "Did you know you did
that—undressed like that?" I pursued. The fatigue and distrac-
tion from my long night with Cynthia Waterford and concerns
about Oubre faded.

"No, no idea. I think I got kinda confused. And they all
acted strange toward me. Tim almost dragged me out the door,
asking what got into me, and nothing upsets him." Indeed,
there he sat impassively.

"Have you gotten confused like that other times?"

"More than I want to remember. People tell me I sometimes
walk into a room and ask things like 'Who am I?' or 'Where am
I?' But I never recall that."

"You're not aware you do this?"

"Not until they tell me," she said softly. "Sometimes they say
I rub my thighs and chest and talk nonsense. I did that in

church once when I was a kid, during my brother's wedding. Mom nearly killed me later, but I swear I wasn't trying to be funny."

Trying not to feed any new symptoms into her menagerie of complaints, I began to piece together an incredible story. For over twelve years, Carol Barge had at least once a week experienced feelings of dissociation from the world around her. Just as often, she experienced a dreamy ripple of déjà vu, as if she had already done exactly whatever she was doing then. Sometimes she'd experience a giddy sense of fear, similar to her childhood anxiety about falling off a fast-moving bicycle or roller coaster, when there was nothing to fear. She would lose track of a conversation or become perplexed by a break in the continuity of a television program. Sometimes, she urinated in her pants, the last time while rear-ending an automobile. Carol had not discussed her incontinence or dreamy states with anyone since her family doctor had called her an overly emotional teenager and prescribed an antibiotic in case a urinary infection was causing her bladder to leak. Mrs. Barge admitted that she had shied away from social contacts and work since leaving high school and felt especially insecure after the couple left Elmira because of her fears of embarrassing herself.

Tim Barge was a dazed voyeur to his wife's admissions. I moved a few steps toward him and prodded, "Have you noticed any peculiar behavior in Carol, something she might not be aware of?"

"I think so. I mean something she said herself," he burst out, then glanced at his wife apologetically. He told me about several episodes in which Carol had stared blankly, smacked her lips, and repetitively brushed her chest for about a half minute. Afterward, she had acted confused. She had these little spells since high school, but he figured she was high-strung or deep in thought. But even he was shocked three years ago when Carol had one and then urinated on herself as they waited for a table in a restaurant.

He wondered if something that happened two months ago

might mean anything. He had awakened at 5:00 A.M. because their bed was shaking. He turned to Carol just as the movement stopped and saw her staring blankly at the ceiling. Her breathing was imperceptible. He touched her face and called her name over and over until he was almost shouting. Thinking that her heart had stopped (why, he thought, hadn't the doctors believed her when she had complained about chest pain?), he leaped to his knees, thumped her chest, and started CPR. Within seconds, she grabbed his hair and neck, struggling to push away the air he forced into her mouth. They both sat up startled. She jumped from bed and walked into the kitchen before he could speak. Neither of them mentioned the incident until the evening, when Tim inquired meekly if Carol had felt an earthquake that morning. She recalled nothing.

Now the woman made some sense to me. She was not, at least not entirely, a malingerer or a hypochondriac on a kamikaze mission against doctors. She clutched onto symptoms such as pain and dizziness because no one recognized her real symptoms as a disease. Since childhood, Carol Barge had unknowingly suffered from epilepsy.

Her attacks, called psychomotor seizures, emanated from the part of the brain that deals with emotion and memory. An electrical storm of discharges from the neurons in one of the brain's temporal lobes, those banana-shaped convolutions of cortex set like thumbs stretching forward along each side of the cerebral hemisphere's fist, caused her unwilled thoughts and actions. If the storm, like the funnel of a tornado, spread to the adjacent cortex, simple zombielike actions, confusion, and amnesia followed. An entire seizure would resolve in the time it took to undress in front of friends, empty her bladder in public, or rear-end a car.

Epileptic spells that arise in and near the temporal lobes have fascinated witnesses since words were first recorded. More than one prophet probably received his inspiration from these electrical storms. Hippocrates was among the first to suggest that the trances implied disease, not divine intervention. Dostoevsky, whose father and uncle were physicians in Moscow, tried to control his seizures with bromides, the first occasionally useful therapy.

I explained my diagnosis to the Barges and urged Carol to take an anticonvulsant drug called Tegretol.

"You mean," she said bitterly, "I've been brain damaged all my life and no one did anything?"

I tried to reassure her. "There's nothing to suggest brain damage. Over one percent of Americans have epilepsy. That's more than two million people, and a quarter of them have psychomotor spells like yours. Some get it from infections, tumors, or strokes. For some, it seems to be an inherited predisposition. But most younger patients like you often have a scar from trauma at birth to the temporal lobe's memory-processing center, the hippocampus. It's a tiny area of injury that doesn't get worse; but in ways we don't fully understand, the injury makes nerve cells overly excitable. We'll do some tests to be certain nothing more serious is going on. The anticonvulsant medication will help suppress the electrical excitability from around the scar and take care of your spells."

I felt certain I could control her seizures, so I did not mention brain surgery. Patients who fail on drugs often die from accidents during a trance or even commit suicide. So at U.C.L.A. and a half-dozen other centers, neurologists and neurosurgeons bore holes into the skull and push thin electroencephalogram wires in and around each temporal lobe. Then they record the EEG waves from each wire until they have fished out exactly where the flurry of spike-shaped discharges that arise with a seizure are located. Recently, a technique called positron emission tomography, the PET scan, has less invasively revealed the hidden focus. Radioactive sugar injected into the bloodstream is taken up by nerve cells in an amount roughly proportional to how active they are. When the head is scanned, the PET machine produces images of the brain based on the activity of its neurons. A temporal-lobe scar is revealed because it appears inactive and cold between seizures. But during a psychomotor seizure, neurons become hot with the rapid metabolism that sustains the electrical tornado's discharge. In about half these patients the injury is located in a place where the neurosurgeon can safely lop it off and cure the epilepsy.

I asked Carol Barge and her husband to keep a diary of any peculiar spells until she completed her tests and returned in two weeks. "I'm not going to be spied on," she announced angrily.

"It's nothing malicious," I cajoled. "I need an outside observer to pick up on any seizures that you aren't aware of." She stared out the window.

I wondered if her symptoms had produced private meanings and feelings unknowable to anyone but herself. There was no way to tell whether the discharges from one of her temporal lobes might have been producing a lifetime of messages that translated into the oddities of her thinking and personality. The injury in her brain may have produced a kind of blind spot like the one in her vision, which her mind had to fill in to maintain her own particular sense of reality. Indeed, epileptics whose seizure discharge originates around the left temporal lobe tend to be overly controlled and reflective. Those with a right-sided electrical storm tend to be impulsive, aggressive, and moody. I would bet that Carol's electrical spikes arose from the right.

AFTER SEEING OUBRE, who was so dry that his skin had taken on a milky glaze, ready to crack into epidermal cobblestones, I stopped by the neurology ward on One West. Mavis Roberts, the head nurse for the past fifteen years, greeted me with a hug and a request for baby pictures. At the far end of the hall, the ward residents and nurses, together with the social worker who served as the troupe's Jewish mother, had begun their slow-paced rounds.

In the same sly and dutiful fashion in which she had manipulated generations of egotistical residents for their own good, Mavis said, "You know, they're going to round on one of your old friends. Remember Greg Forbes?"

"Greg's here? Is it anything serious?"

"Just a little aspiration. You should say hello, if you have time."

In the first months of my residency, a psychiatry resident asked me to evaluate a young suicidal patient in the emergency room because he looked and sounded "funny." I found Greg

Forbes sprawled out in a stupor, overdosed with alcohol and sedatives. Saliva pooled in his gaping mouth and soaked his shirt and pillow, and a torrent of incoherent words slurred off his shriveled tongue. His hollowed temples and cheeks and wasted hand muscles made it seem as if his skin had imploded into the spaces between his bones. His chart recorded his age as thirty-one.

Greg's cousin Sal, a burly, pink-cheeked electrician in his mid-thirties, held his shoulder as I pushed him on a gurney from the E.R. to One West. Sal said that they had been lovers since they were teenagers. He was afraid that Greg might end up like an uncle who died a skid-row alcoholic in Cincinnati. I reassured him and explained that first I would start antibiotics to treat the pneumonia Greg had acquired from inhaling his own saliva. After everyone got a night's sleep, we'd figure out why he was wasting away.

The next morning, Forbes provided the history he had been too doped to offer at our first meeting. For the past three to four years, Greg had become progessively weaker, his forearm and hand muscles had withered, and his speech had become slurred. Six months ago, when he could no longer use a hammer or a screwdriver, his boss accused him of laziness and drunkenness and fired him. He isolated himself at home, ashamed to socialize because he drooled and because people found his speech barely intelligible. Alcohol helped him sleep but made him choke.

Greg recalled that people had always told him he sounded as if he had a cold. In grade school, he occasionally coughed up milk or soda through his nose. He ran slower than most boys and was not able to hit a baseball hard without losing his grip on a bat. Although he managed a stint in the army as a mechanic, he couldn't handle large wrenches. Greg did not know of anyone else in the family with similar weakness. He had been told that his grandmother and mother, with whom he had little contact after adolescence, died of pneumonia in middle age.

Greg did quite well when I tested his memory, judgment,

language, and his ability to calculate, entirely contradicting the dull-witted appearance created by his insensate facial expression and gurgling, monotone voice. His laugh, high-pitched and weak, barely projected past his lips. And his face looked as smooth as the unnaturally tight skin of a movie star after repeated face lifts. Greg's tongue undulated like a furrowed mound of worms. Bubbly saliva and breakfast-food particles pooled in his throat and overflowed onto his chest. Although he had very little strength in his hands, his arm and leg muscles were still strong. His tendon reflexes were normal and he felt a pinprick, vibration, and change in the position of his toe and finger joints quite normally.

"Greg," I said, "as bad as the alcohol is for you, it isn't the primary cause of your choking and weakness. You probably have a disease that's affecting you someplace along what we call the motor unit—in the nerve cells that send out the signals for movement from the spinal cord and brain stem, or the cables that travel from them out to your muscles, or in the muscles themselves."

"My nerves are bad," he responded glumly. "But Sal got me some tranquilizers and nothing got better."

"I can imagine; but I mean nerves in an anatomic sense, not emotional stress. We'll need to do a series of tests and a muscle biopsy."

"Can anything be done?"

"I don't know enough yet," I answered, guessing that we were unlikely to discover a cure. "We'll look for everything that's treatable."

His blood and x-ray studies were normal. When I stimulated his peripheral nerves with a tiny electrical shock, the impulse traveled without impediment. That eliminated the peripheral nerve as the weak link in his motor units. Electromyography (a test in which tiny needle electrodes are stabbed quickly into various limb muscles to amplify their electrical activity onto an oscilloscope screen) pointed to a disease that primarily affected the nerve cells, rather than the muscle fibers.

We can't, of course, cut out a slice of spinal cord in order to prove beyond a doubt where a problem lies. Instead, we look at what the muscle reflects. The many thousands of fibers that comprise any normal muscle are so small in diameter that fifty of them, lined up, form a queue only one millimeter wide. When a motor neuron in the cord dies, the hundred or more fibers under its command become orphaned and wither.

A microscopic evaluation of small samples of Greg's arm and leg muscles showed shrunken, triangular muscle fibers. Each group of atrophied fibers was almost undoubtedly connected to a sick or dead motor neuron in his spinal cord's gray matter. The findings added up to a form of amyotrophic lateral sclerosis, Lou Gehrig's disease. Senator Jacob Javits, the actor David Niven, and my family doctor, Arthur Krieger, also suffered with ALS.

What intrigued me about Greg Forbes was whether or not his disease ran in the family. Fewer than ten percent of the cases of ALS are hereditary. But his grandmother and mother had both died from pneumonia—the same infection that now threatened him.

I discharged Greg after prescribing an antidepressant medication that would dry up his saliva, as well as lift his spirits. A psychiatrist would also begin to work with him. And, with Greg's approval, I began to trace his family tree. If my hunch about a hereditary basis for his wasting proved correct, we might be able to predict the progression of his specific brand of motor neuron disease, anticipate its complications, and hold it in check until someone came up with a palliative measure or cure.

We do not know why people get ALS. Researchers have looked without success for a specific ALS virus, something like the polio virus that kills only motor neurons. It may be that there's a dock on the outer membrane of the motor neurons of ALS victims that attracts a virus or chemical toxin. Or it might be that the cells contain a genetic defect that eventually produces some kind of time-bomb-like toxic substance. Potentially harmful environmental substances like lead occasionally cause a disease very similar to ALS and raise the possibility that other, less familiar toxins also kill neurons. Neuroscientists are also seeking possible immunological causes. Just as Dick Gallagher had manufactured antibodies meant to incapacitate the virus he had, and that paradoxically attacked his peripheral nerves, Greg's body might be making something that was inadvertently destroying his motor neurons.

His family's death certificates led me to newspaper obituaries stored by state historical societies, to the office records stored in Tulsa of a deceased doctor, and to records from hospitals throughout the Midwest. This genealogical hunt, like a hobbyist's passion for collection, drove me through my entire first year of residency.

Greg's maternal great-great-grandfather in Europe and a great-grandmother in America had both died in their forties from unknown causes. A physician in Oklahoma had written that Greg's maternal grandmother had a speech impediment "which makes her sound like a harelip." Greg's voice might be described in the same way. She had died at age fifty-two of pneumonia and, supposedly, anorexia nervosa. It seemed possible that she choked when she tried to eat, which caused her to starve down to the sixty-three pounds she weighed at death. Her son, Greg's uncle, died at fifty. His hospital records revealed that he had been treated repeatedly for injuries from falls and beatings and that his doctors couldn't understand his speech. He was diagnosed as suffering from malnutrition, syphilis, and alcoholism and was the drunk Sal recalled dying on skid row.

Greg's mother's second husband, a hardware-store owner in Indiana whom Greg had never met, told me over the phone that his wife had grown progressively weak, coughed a lot, refused to eat, and spent her last year bedridden, dying at forty-eight of what the family doctor called tuberculosis. I asked about her voice.

"Had a speech impediment long's I knew her," he said, "as if a clothespin pinched her nose." He also described bouts of choking on liquids. And he remembered authorizing an autopsy.

If Greg's uncle and mother carried his grandmother's genes for a motor-neuron disease like ALS, then it behaved in what is called an autosomal dominant pattern, in which half the off-spring of a victim may end up getting the disease. The widower had two daughters who seemed quite healthy to him. I decided to try and obtain the results of the wife's autopsy before saddling him with the prospect that his children might be at risk.

A month later, I received the autopsy report on Greg's mother. Her lungs were found to be stiff with the pus of a severe pneumonia, but her brain and spinal cord "appeared normal" to the pathologist's naked eye. When I examined the slides of her tissues microscopically to find the evidence I sought, I saw that she died with only a third of the normal number of motor neurons in her brain stem and spinal cord, and most of these looked sick. And the slides showed her turquoise and pink-stained muscles had shrunk, just like Greg's. I then knew, without any doubt, that Greg suffered with a variant of ALS that had been programmed into his genes.

Greg's family's disease had behaved in a clear-cut pattern in the grandmother, mother, and uncle. Their death certificates consistently recorded the cause of death as pneumonia, but what really happened was that they couldn't care for themselves with their withered arms and legs, expand their chests to breathe, swallow without choking exhaustively, and communicate their needs and horror. As they smothered in their own secretions, their minds remained sound, making them helpless witnesses of their dissolution.

Greg returned to the neurology clinic a week after I had reviewed his mother's autopsy specimens. He seemed less depressed and had stopped drinking beer.

"Did you ever get the stuff on my mother?" he asked. I wondered if he could handle confirmation of the suspicion I only once raised to him. My excitement in chronicling his disease suddenly vanished. "I've got what she had, don't I?"

"Your mother's autopsy shows the nerve-cell degeneration we talked about," I conceded. "Her brother had the same problem."

"So I'm going to die?" His smooth, doll's face became wet with tears.

"We can keep the disease at bay much longer than they were able to," I said, handing him a box of tissues, "by anticipating the complications that might arise. Besides, these hereditary diseases vary in the extent to which they affect each succeeding generation."

"Then there's nothing to do."

I put my hand on his shoulder, but he backed away as if I'd hurt him. I wanted to offer Greg hope and pass some responsibility for his future into his control. And I wanted to feel less guilty about how my search had backfired for him.

"You must keep up your nutrition and stay away from beer. Years from now you might need minor surgery to fix your swallowing muscles, or we might have to pass a thin tube into your stomach to feed you. And you've got to follow through on the exercise program we set up to strengthen the muscle fibers of the nerve cells that still work. That'll help you compensate. I will watch for any new discoveries. There's a lot of research going on to find the causes for neuromuscular diseases like yours." I wouldn't hear from him for nearly six months, until Sal insisted he return.

In the interim, I called Greg's mother's second husband again in Indiana. A young woman with a nasal voice answered the phone. She did not have to introduce herself. She barely remembered her mother, but joked that her daddy always said she reminded him of his wife when they married. I asked her to see a neurologist at a nearby university hospital as part of a research project we were doing on Greg.

Greg's sister from his mother's first marriage visited from Santa Barbara to find out more about her brother's condition. I was, of course, anxious to see if she shared his affliction, especially since, if she did, she might want to consider whether or

not to bear children who could carry her potentially cata-
strophic genes.

Myra downplayed what she called her husky voice and dis-
missed the importance of the choking spells she had several
times a month, mostly after a few evening cocktails. Electromyography showed subtle electrical abnormalities in her arm
muscles that were much like Greg's.

I wasn't sure that I had the right to inform her of her risk
without her somehow choosing to know. One of my professors
at U.C.L.A. had pointed out that although there is a test that
can identify which of the still-unaffected children of parents
who suffer with Huntington's Chorea, so-called Woody
Guthrie's disease, may get it later in life, about half of those offered it refuse the test.

Reluctantly, I told Myra what I had learned. She handled
the possibility she might carry her mother's disease, to a degree
of severity not predictable, with little outward concern. But
within a year, she started drinking herself into nightly stupors.
Psychiatric intervention failed. Greg told me she believed her
ability to swallow had worsened. Near the end of my residency,
she committed suicide.

All the time that I treated him, Greg discussed only his
symptoms and exercise program with me, never his grief.
Maybe unlocking his genetic secret made me a part of his anguish. And then I too withdrew emotionally from Greg. I carried too much guilt.

But at Mavis's urging, I went in to see Greg for the first time
in five years. My reluctance evaporated as soon as he greeted
me in his muffled, now almost unintelligible voice. His face was
frozen, not even a snarl. Jutting bone fenced in oblong and
triangular troughs at his temples, cheeks, and hands. But he
took a few brisk strides toward me and seemed pleased that I
visited. Then he asked if I thought he was better.

"Better? Hard to remember exactly what you were like last
time," I equivocated. "You're at least holding your own."

"Yeah?" When I could not understand his next comment, he
wrote clumsily, "Better than others in the family."

* * *

My office schedule that morning passed swiftly until Rene, my secretary, sneaked in Harvey Block, who claimed he had to be seen immediately.

"Morning, Dr. Dolkins," Harvey exclaimed. With a few quick lashes of his tongue and a flourish of finger twitches, he added, "Who's the alcky in the waiting room? Guy's real shaky." Harvey referred to a hunched-over man with Parkinson's. "Had a friend like that I bowled with . . ."

"Mr. Block," I interrupted. Harvey's irrelevant remarks were as welcome as a business-reply card falling out of a magazine. "How are you doing? Did the medicine decrease the tingling sensations in your feet?"

"It helps some," Harvey answered, "especially when I sleep, but the wife still nags me about the wiggling. You ever get your heavy wool socks wet in the snow with your boots tied too tight? Feet are kinda feeling like that."

He removed his slippers and socks. The odor of his feet filled the room. Then he flickered his toes, slid off the exam table, and stepped delicately, as if traversing a slippery puddle of mud. When he got beside me he surveyed my scalp, not unlike an anteater about to poke into a giant ant hill, and observed, "Well look at that. You're losing it on top, all right. Going bald, I'd say." I decided to turn him around.

"How much did you drink this week?"

"I didn't really drink," he said, rolling his eyes beneath thick, gray brows and raising his left hand. The calcified tendons in the palm curled his fingers like a papal hand in benediction. "You can't always . . ."

"Did you drink wine or beer?" I pursued. Harvey had quit Alcoholics Anonymous because he claimed no one let him finish his thoughts.

"Well," he began, "I had problems. My penis shrunk up." I yielded to the inevitable, prolonged siege. "Back in the army in '41," he said pensively, perhaps readying himself to bare every detail at weekly intervals since, "a corpsman or doctor used to do a short-arm inspection after a three-day pass." I must have looked puzzled, so he added, "You see, he inspects your pecker and whatchacallit, says milk it down. When he eyeballs mine, he says, 'You got a flat.' Now I didn't have much sticking out then. So the corpsman, he listed it as a flat. Some nerve controls it, I learnt from a buddy at the movie theater where I worked." Harvey repeatedly drew a circle on his thigh, as if running the index finger over the lip of a cocktail glass. "People think being a projectionist is easy. I tell you it can be kinda queer. That was after fifteen years in the furnace-repair business. Never shoulda left that. 'Course, it was okay with sex then," he added with thumbs and toes snapping, "but now I'm having trouble getting my nuts off. Some of those adult movies . . ."

My mind began to reel as he went on and on. Harvey's brain contained the odds and ends of a kitchen junk drawer, the place where old keys, chewed pencils, a magnifying glass, and assorted screws and connectors rest, ready for plucking if needed. Most of us add to the drawer's treasures, but rarely re-examine them.

After a circuitous interrogation, I determined that Harvey could not maintain an erection for intercourse, probably because his alcoholic neuropathy sapped the autonomic-nerve supply to his penis. The sympathetic and parasympathetic peripheral nerves of the autonomic or self-regulating system oppose and modulate each other as they supply the organs, glands, and blood vessels of the body. To achieve and maintain an erection, the autonomic system must be stimulated to continuously increase blood flow into the spongy tissue to the penis. Because the axons of the autonomic nerves, driven in part by the hypothalamus and temporal lobes, travel long distances from the brain stem and spinal cord, they are subject to toxic insults. Erection and ejaculation are often among the first casualties.

"How long have you had this problem?" I asked.

"I'll be honest with you. Some time. Maybe a year or two," he said dolefully. As with his drinking, he had denied impotence when I first saw him.

"Mr. Block," I suggested, "see if you and the wife can engage in more foreplay." I wasn't about to tell someone with six decades of private thoughts about what sex is supposed to be, especially not a man I imagined jabbering and twitching away in bed, which techniques to try, unless he asked. "And relax. Don't put pressure on yourself to perform. You've been married forty-five years. She'll understand. But if you keep drinking, your penis may never inflate."

"Yeah, when I worry, it don't work at all. But she's not an easy woman. She's nudged it on occasion before, but she's from farm country. Did I tell you about her school reunion?"

I checked my watch—twenty minutes had passed. No time for more clutter. "If things don't work out," I said, "we can discuss a penile prosthesis and a different drug for your numbness. See you in a month."

As I dictated my report to his internist, Harvey popped back through the doorway.

"Dr. Dokkins, can I see you for just a minute?" he asked, flossing a back molar with the cellophane from a pack of Camels. "One thing, real important." I walked into the hall expectantly.

"Secretary's putting the drinker in the exam room," he began, inhaling his chest full, as if ready to strut about with his worldly observation about my trembling Parkinson's patient. I was sure he was about to plead for help with his alcohol abuse. "You see, I got this problem with flabulating like crazy."

"Flabulating?"

"Yeah." He moved closer, his belly almost touching my elbow. "Every time I set on the toilet, all hell breaks loose. And the little ones when you're walking down the street embarrasses the wife. When she isn't telling me to stop wiggling my toes, she's sniffing after me. Think it's the napopathy of my nerves?"

"No," I said coldly, but Harvey's charmingly solemn manner reduced me to an affectionate smile.

"I eat a lotta fruit. A friend of mine from back in . . ."

"That can cause flatulence. Try eating less and make your wife happy."

"Now there's an idea." He walked a few steps to the entrance of our waiting room, by our secretaries' desks, and called back, "And I'll tell her about the foreplay."

At lunchtime, Sandy Waterford walked into the doctors' dining room at Freeman and everyone hushed uneasily. A few of his colleagues by the coffee pots quietly extended their best wishes. A heart surgeon to my left leaned toward me with raised brows and asked, "Would you have saved her that night if you had to do it over again?"

"Of course." Wouldn't he resuscitate a young woman? "We didn't have all the facts when she was helicoptered in, so I couldn't make a certain prognosis, and now that I think I can, she's too stable to withdraw any measures. Besides, we didn't save her—the people on Catalina did."

"Well, she's not gonna make it, is she?"

"You mean survive? She'll probably live indefinitely. And somehow Sandy will survive that."

Sandy saw me leaving and asked if we could check Cynthia. As we walked to an elevator, he said earnestly, "What did you think of that list I gave you? I mean, there's not much hard scientific proof any would work, but . . . I don't know."

Culled from newspaper and magazine clippings, experimental animal studies, and word-of-mouth suppositions, his library research turned up the familiar, desperate, often absurd interventions that my patients with brain injuries and incurable diseases like ALS, multiple sclerosis, and Alzheimer's dementia frequently uncover. People with real and imagined ailments spend over $10 billion a year on pet therapies as diverse as ionizing boards, chelation, over-the-counter pills and salves, and hyperbaric oxygen, and some even undergo dental work to replace their old amalgam fillings with something perceived to be less toxic than mercury. When traditional medicine fails, some even march to offbeat clinics that serve hope along with expensive potions, megavitamins, and gimcracks reminiscent of a traveling tonic-salesman's wares. The victim's panic and doctor's helpless frustration lead legitimate medical researchers to try vitamins, steroids, hormones, toxic chemotherapy, antiviral agents, snake venoms, transfusions, plasmapheresis like Gallagher's, and, in problems like Cynthia Waterford's, drugs that alter cerebral chemical transmissions and blood flow. Nothing yet heals brain injuries with even occasional success.

I tried to be responsive to Sandy's anxiety. "We still don't have any therapies to help the neurons damaged by cerebral anoxia from a cardiac arrest or drowning. It's complicated even trying to figure out what exactly causes cell destruction. Sure, vitamins C and E on your list may neutralize some of the harmful substances that a neuron produces soon after injury. But even if we fed them to Cynthia while she was in the hyperbaric chamber, blood flow to transport them might not have been adequate to reach the cortex, or her neurons might have been too sick to take them up."

"Some of the things on the list increase blood flow," he argued.

"Any treatment must be given in the first minutes, and maybe someday in the first hours, after cardiac standstill."

"What about now?" Sandy pleaded. "There must be something we can do. Maybe the papaverine can help. Everybody uses it, especially the older doctors on the staff."

And they use it for everything. I thought—stroke, mild memory loss, dementia—because it supposedly increases blood flow to the brain. Even if it did, a brief increase in flow does not mean that a neuron will work better. Healthy nerve cells extract what they need from blood even at half the normal rate of flow. Still, there's comfort in hope. "Okay, I'll start her on it by a feeding tube, with vitamins."

In the ICU, Sandy hurried to his wife's side. He leaned across the respirator's tubes, placed a set of headphones over her ears and wired them to a pocket-size tape recorder. "Just some messages from the kids and some of our favorite music—some sixties rock, 'Norwegian Wood,' some jazz and a few classical works. Think Cynthia can hear it?"

"Her auditory-evoked response looked pretty good yesterday.

That was the test where we pasted wires to her scalp that were connected to a computer and then made clicking noises in her ears. The sounds are transmitted as electrical signals along the auditory nerve, into the brain stem and up to the temporal-lobe cortex where sound's appreciated and finally interpreted. The computer picks up the signals as they pass along successive groups of neurons. We can't tell if the rest of her brain makes sense of sounds, but I can say that your music will arrive in the right place."

"Great. Her parents are coming in from Miami and would want to know, too. I know this seems a little crazy," he added with a sheepish grin, "but I'm going up north this weekend to a retreat. They say you can meditate in an isolation chamber and, if you're good at it, communicate by telepathy. Guess it's like a séance. I mean, it's worth a try, isn't it, if Cyn's trying to tell us something?"

PART 2

Something entered people, something
chopped, pressed, punctured, had its
way with them and if you looked, bad
child, it entered you.

MAXINE KUMIN,
"The Man of Many L's"

SEVEN

TWO DAYS AGO, Ethel Oubre had seemed about to un-
ravel.

"It's just not right to prolong Larry's life when he's
like this." She rubbed her hands on her slacks. "He wouldn't
want it."

"It's always difficult to tell what someone in his situation
would choose. Hang in with him. I believe he has turned the
corner." She must have realized that, must have seen his improvement—taking in more fluid, breathing on his own though
still intubated. Perhaps she was afraid about their future, not
the present.

Today, two weeks after his stroke, Oubre was stable enough
for extubation. But buzzards had as much business hovering
over him as docs and nurses. Intravenous and nasogastric tubes
fed him, a catheter in his bladder emptied him, and his eyes
were as opaque as pond water stirred up with bottom mud. As
soon as the intern slipped out the airway pipe, Larry spoke a
few hoarse, unintelligible words. Then he saw me. He stretched

his right arm as if awakening, raised his hand, and flashed me a victory sign with his thumb and first finger. I could have kissed him. "Show off for Ethel and your son," I told him. "I know you'll be okay."

I had moved Cynthia Waterford from the ICU at Daniel Freeman to a medical ward, since she no longer needed to be on a respirator. When one of her nurses told me that Mrs. Waterford had looked at her during the morning sponge bath, I mumbled a disbelieving "really?" and marched to her private room, chart in hand.

Dozens of cards and bouquets of flowers cluttered walls and tabletops. A sheet of drawing paper folded into quarters and taped to a lacquered closet door stated in red crayon, "FOR MOMMY." Inside, the message continued;

> *Mommys come and mommys go*
> *But your the best mom*
> *We ever know*
> *Camp is great.*
> *Please get better,*

THE KIDS

I wondered what Sandy had told them.

Cynthia lay in a light blue nightgown with her eyes open and lips slightly apart. A thin, clear-plastic nasogastric feeding tube dangled from one nostril. She sank into the foamy peaks and recesses of an egg-crate mattress designed to protect her from getting pressure sores. Aside from an occasional reflexive extension of her arms and legs, she showed no more brain function than the photograph of her daughters on her nightstand. Cynthia's nurse wished that her charge were better, so she had overinterpreted the patient's neutrally aimed eyes. The day before, I had told her parents that there was a slim chance she might improve beyond the point where she would be more than minimally aware of her surroundings. But I knew there could never be a victory sign here.

I reached Dick Gallagher's room on the rehabilitation wing as his nurse drew a yellow curtain in front of his bed. Sharon fiddled with a roll of toilet paper. Dick sat on a commode chair. "Hey," he called. "I could feel my leg muscles hold some of my weight when the nurse helped me shift from the bed to this pot."

"Great. I'm getting good reports about you." Remarkably, in one week he had regained the strength to move his shoulder and hip muscles slightly and sit up without toppling over.

"Working my ass off. How long will it take?" Urine splashed against the gray plastic bowl under his seat.

"It depends on how long your peripheral nerves take to heal and reconnect to their muscle fibers. In the meantime, you have to build up your endurance, keep your skin and joints in good shape, and strengthen the muscle fibers that still twitch." He passed an unfragrant bowel movement and I promptly waved good-bye.

From the doorway of a corner room down the hall, I looked in on a man in his early sixties called Duke by his close friends. His white hair was thicker than one might expect after a full course of radiation. The tension in his forehead muscles persisted even though his eyes were closed. A spy novel lay across his chest. His dinner tray appeared untouched. He awakened, as if sensing my presence.

"Didn't eat anything?" I asked after I walked in and lifted the gold plastic cover off his plate of chicken, mashed potatoes, and lima beans.

"Not hungry. Had half the tuna sandwich left over from last night," he said, then grimaced as he lifted his legs over the side of his bed and sat up.

"I hear you're still putting away quite a few candy bars every day."

"Where'd you hear that?" He nearly smiled.

"One of your smugglers, a nurse you must have bribed with charm." He ignored me as he usually did when I talked about his diet. Duke's appetite for food had disappeared two or three years ago. He lived mostly on chocolate and canned tuna at home. "How'd your therapy go today? Is your balance any better?"

He squinted and clenched his jaw. "Everything's about the same." Sadness, like the moist heat from a steam press, rose around us. I had used every trick I knew to get him better and I was failing. And he expected that.

Five years ago, he had slipped and fallen on the wet pavement of a shopping mall and bruised his low back and right shoulder. A classic workaholic and an intensely private man, Duke ignored the pain for months and said nothing about it until one day he caught sight of his reflection in a storefront window, "hobbling like an old man." His family physician sent him to an orthopedic surgeon who hospitalized him for possible pinched nerves in his neck and back. Duke had always regretted reporting the pain. More than once he had said, "That bastard stretched my neck and back with sandbag weights on pulleys, like I was a shrunken rug that he'd wanted to fit wall-to-wall. It was worse than the pain, and everything's been downhill since."

After he refused further rack treatments, a neurologist examined him and agreed that a disc in his low back had ruptured and was pinching one of the nerves that runs through the spine there. Duke decided against further bed rest and limped back to work.

Several months later, he caught his right foot on a doorway threshold and went sprawling to the floor. His wife, Gladys, and the G.P. begged him to get another opinion, so he submitted to an evaluation by a highly recommended neurologist. Duke complained about pain in his neck, numbness in his right arm and leg, and low-back pain that ran down both legs when he walked. The neurologist concluded that Duke suffered from a lumbar radiculopathy and cervical myelopathy; one disc pinched a nerve in his low back and another pressed against the spinal cord in his neck.

Doctors prescribed a neck collar, bed rest, analgesics for pain, muscle relaxants, and tranquilizers. The drugs made Duke confused, disoriented, and delusional, and only after an arduous hospitalization were the side effects cleaned up. At home, Gladys grew desperate. She repeatedly called her eldest son—a doctor—and asked his advice, but he said that he had discussed the case with the physicians close to Duke and believed their approach—to try to avoid surgery on his neck and back—made sense. "But you don't know," she said. "He tells them his hand's numb and he feels clumsy walking and they give him pills he won't take. I'm not overreacting. You don't see him tripping and forgetting—he looks so old all of a sudden."

Nearly a year after his first fall, Duke phoned his son and told him that while shaving that morning, he had felt a peculiar numbness in his right cheek, as if he'd been injected with novocaine. Without pausing for a moment, without explanation, Duke's son insisted over his father's objections that he fly immediately to Los Angeles. The next day, he admitted Duke to the U.C.L.A. Medical Center.

The first test, a CT scan, showed that a deep-seated, white-stippled ball filled the thalamus on the left side of Duke's brain. The partly calcified mass, benign-looking as a child's fist, accounted for every last misdiagnosed symptom.

A neuroradiologist, one of those bright, succinct, usually emotionless faculty members who rarely makes eye contact when he speaks, watched me closely as I held Duke's x-ray films against an opaque, white fluorescent screen. Computers whirred reels of magnetic tape all around us.

"It's a tumor, all right," he said. "Calcified glioma. Maybe an oligodendroglioma, unlikely to be a vascular malformation since it doesn't light up with dye. Is this a relative?" he asked, peering at the name at the scan's upper-right corner.

"My father."

"Sorry." The radiologist paused while I ran my fingers over

the smooth black film until they stopped on the clumped dots of the white mass. "He's from back east?" I nodded. "Did the symptoms just start?"

"They've been there a year or so," I answered, trying to act as if this were just another case. "No one thought about a problem in his head because neck and back pain were his main complaint. Ironically, I probably inhibited his neurologist from getting a CT scan; he was more academic, more cautious in his approach than he'd have been with a patient who wasn't the father of a neurologist. Anyway, is there a chance this is an old hematoma or vascular malformation?"

"Maybe; not likely. Well, maybe."

"Let's do an arteriogram to be more certain. I've got to tell him and get someone here to look after him. I shouldn't be in charge. You can't be objective." He nodded, studying the computer keyboard.

Outside Duke's window, a cold February rain fell. He snoozed on his back with his arms raised along the sides of his head in a football referee's touchdown sign. There's a photo taken by Gladys in 1949 of Duke and me, side by side, sleeping in precisely this position. It won a drugstore-sponsored prize of twenty-five dollars. My mother leaned forward from her high-backed chair as I sat down on the edge of Duke's hospital bed. He opened his eyes and asked, "What's up?"

"Dad, I went over the CT scan," I began, holding myself together. "There's something serious going on, something that may be growing in your brain." He made no response.

"My God, what's growing in his brain?" Gladys rasped, pressing clenched fists against her chest.

I tried to prepare them, but tears burst from me. I grabbed his cold hand. "Daddy. I'm so sorry. You have a brain tumor, a slowly growing brain tumor." He looked into my face a few moments until he grasped what I meant. With more composure, I said, "We'll do everything possible to treat it. It might be something that can be cured."

"I don't get it," he said, massaging his jaw. "My back and leg hurt. That's what bothers me. My head . . ."

"The head's what's caused trouble walking. Then your falls made your back and neck hurt. The numbness is from the brain, not your neck or back. But once we decide what's best for the head, I promise we'll take care of the back and leg pain. I know what that's about and we'll fix it."

Duke's blue gray eyes narrowed, his square jaw set below clenched teeth. For the time, his decisions were left to me.

The next day, Bernard Dobkin introduced himself as "Duke" to the actor John Wayne while they waited in the radiology suite for their x-ray tests. The Hollywood hero, dying of cancer, asked what my father was in for. "Back trouble. Nothing serious," he replied.

The cerebral arteriogram, a test in which a liquid dye is injected through a catheter fed from an artery in the groin up to the arteries in the neck to create a picture of the brain's circulatory system, revealed neither the wormy blood vessels of a vascular malformation nor the wild, misshapen arteries usually found within a highly malignant tumor. Duke's tumor probably grew from either the astrocytes or oligodendrocytes—the supporting glial cells that surround neurons. We could not biopsy it, because it was too deep to safely reach.

A procession of consultants, chairmen of their departments in neurology, neurosurgery, and orthopedic surgery, visited Duke on One West and suggested that the brain lesion should be treated with radiation and the back with medications. But a trial of drugs at U.C.L.A. either produced an allergic rash or grayed out his mind until he grew somnolent and disoriented. I had failed in my promise to relieve his pain. Duke insisted that we find out why his back hurt, so I cajoled his doctors to order a myelogram.

The study, in which a liquid injected into the spinal fluid outlines the nerve roots on x-ray film, is usually done when surgery on the back or neck is contemplated. Most surgeons would be reluctant to operate on the spine of a brain-tumor victim whose lifespan is in doubt; and I would never have ordered the study on an ordinary patient.

The myelogram revealed precisely what his symptoms suggested. Duke had a spinal stenosis, a narrowing of the bony canal in the lower spine that surrounds the nerve roots before they head down to the legs. The nerve roots normally float like a handful of asparagus tips in a glass of water. Duke's were so compressed that they had no room to move. When he walked, his ligaments crunched them, causing pain to radiate from his back into his legs. We could relieve the pain by cutting open the back wall of several vertebrae to allow the nerves some breathing room. But no one operates for pain relief when a brain tumor threatens life.

Duke returned to Philadelphia under the care of another neurology department chairman, who sent him to the best radiation-therapy expert he knew. They decided to use high-energy radiation emitted from a device called a linear accelerator to try and destroy as much of his tumor as possible. Electrons generated by the linear accelerator ride, like surfers, on the crests of radiowaves until they slam into their target—a piece of gold foil. As gold electrons scatter, they're focused and aimed at a target on the patient. The gold electrons penetrate the skull and brain tissue until they knock other electrons off the molecules in the targeted tissue. This wreaks havoc with the replicating machinery, the DNA and RNA, of a dividing cell, enough to destroy it before its nucleus splits into two more cells. Duke's doctors planned to use the maximum amount of radiation they could before normal neurons and glial cells also became overdosed. But radiation almost never cured these tumors. At best, it killed a large percentage of their cells, and those that survived would continue their malicious multiplication.

The six-week course of radiation not only brought on the usual side effects of hair loss and apathy, but dried out Duke's salivary glands and killed his sense of taste to the point where he lost all appetite. When his weight loss and pain drove him further downhill, he was hospitalized for more medications and tests, which made him even more confused. He lost control of his bladder and became fixated on his inability to have a bowel movement. Gladys called: "He's dying. The doctors examine him—I think he's trained their entire residency class in brain tumors—and do nothing."

I talked with his doctors and called my mother. "Take him home, even if you need a nurse there. Feed him whatever he wants—tuna, chocolate bars, anything. We'll fly him out here if things don't get better."

A month later, when Duke came off the plane in Los Angeles in a wheelchair, I was astonished by how much he had changed. His mind wandered. He'd forget that he was in L.A. and that my mother had stayed in Philadelphia. He seemed cheerless and depressed. And he walked like a stroke victim; right arm slightly flexed into his chest, he swung his right leg like he was trying to kick a can on the floor toward the tip of his left foot.

I sent him to the pain management unit at Daniel Freeman. He began a behavioral modification program, which stressed psychological adaptation to chronic pain, and tapered off the codeine he had begun to use with increasing frequency. Biofeedback and counseling trained him to relax and helped increase his tolerance for his neck and back pain. The muscle aches in his neck and shoulders (brought on partly by the way the tumor made him walk) improved with massage and physical therapy. Duke's therapists tried to help him walk with better balance, but the back and leg pain he experienced at every step intensified his depression. So we tried an antidepressant drug, which we hoped would help lift his sadness and apathy, while at the same time increase the concentration in his brain of a neurotransmitter called serotonin, which inhibits pain messages. But the drugs dried out what little saliva the radiation had spared and caused him greater confusion. The combination of tumor and any medication that worked on brain chemistry seemed to cloud his mind.

Back surgery was the only chance he had for pain relief. If he could walk freely, maybe he'd throw off his depression. I had to gather some evidence that the tumor was not visibly growing, which might make Duke feel better and give me the ammunition to insist on surgery for his spinal stenosis.

I asked a colleague at U.C.L.A. who was involved in developing positron emission tomography to scan my father. PET gives us a picture of the brain's blood flow and metabolism. He injected harmless, radioactive glucose into Duke. Neurons use the sugar for their energy needs. The radioactive atom in the glucose emits particles that travel a short distance within the brain, then combine with a nearby electron to produce gamma rays. These are measured by computerized detectors that produce an image of the brain at work.

To my relief, the tumor bed in Duke's thalamus revealed less blood flow and consumption of glucose than the normal brain around it. This meant that the mass was not a "hot" area of growth, but a cool, slowly (if at all) reproducing nest of presumably malignant cells. Indeed, it may have been there for many years. What disturbed me was that the PET scan revealed that Duke's left thalamus and the outer ribbon of cortex in his left frontal, temporal, and parietal lobes were also relatively cold compared to the same brain structures on the right.

The thalamus is an egg-shaped mass of gray matter that sits on top of the brain stem in the middle of the underside of each cerebral hemisphere. Highly organized tiers of neurons here, like the seeds within the compartments of a pomegranate, receive and integrate all the body's sensory information from skin, joints, tendons, muscles, eyes, ears, tongue, and the internal organs. It also handles the constant flurry of signals from the reticular activating system, which keeps the brain alert, and from the hypothalamus, which helps trigger emotional responses. Thalamic neurons then relay these messages to the cortex.

Duke's electrical switchboard had shorted out in its usual physiologic task of driving his left hemisphere to action. His increasing apathy, lack of motivation, inattention, difficulty with memory, confusion, and susceptibility of his thinking to the side effects of drugs were linked in part to a thalamus that hardly sparked. My father's depression, so out of character, was not only a reaction to all the negative experiences and pain he endured, but physiologic, electrochemical.

When I told Duke that his tumor appeared inactive, he looked no less dejected and said, "That sounds okay. But if I could just stop hurting."

After I discussed with his doctors in Philadelphia what we'd found on the PET scan, Duke returned home and underwent back surgery. His neurosurgeon unroofed the backs of three vertebrae so that his nerve roots could float freely in the spinal fluid. When he recovered, most of the pain Duke experienced when walking stopped. But his gait remained awkward and the numbness on his right side persisted. "Am I ever going to get well?" he asked on one of my visits. "Keep walking with the physical therapists and things will improve," I said hopefully.

For two years, Duke almost never complained unless I pressed him. Gladys's play-by-play description of one crisis after another became my only insight into what was going on: falls leading to rib fractures and exacerbations of his neck and low-back pain and bouts of severe headaches that led to more CT scans to see if the tumor had grown. It had not. To my mother's unending dismay, he kept insisting he needed a station wagon so he might return to work, even though pain flared up whenever he drove and his concentration had worsened to the point that he was not safe behind the wheel. Duke was especially upset by his lapses in memory. He would lose words on the tip of his tongue, stutter when trying to recall something that recently took place, attribute what happened to one acquaintance to someone else, and fumble in the once-familiar task of repairing a faucet or electrical switch around the house. Every loss, real but often overblown, further weighted his depression. On the telephone, I listened and made suggestions and spoke with hope, but I barely held their despair at bay.

My parents forced me to move from son to consultant, not because their doctors weren't competent, but because they withheld the support the couple craved. I began to listen more closely to the minor symptoms of all my patients and asked how they and their families were coping with their neurologic disease. The nagging little symptoms of no real medical consequence, which I had tended in the past to ignore or play down, I now took the time to explain. I learned to treat, with a doctor's convincing words, any peculiar tingle or vague light-headedness or transient pain as thoroughly as I treated cerebral herniation.

In the midst of Duke's deterioration, Barbara became pregnant. He decided to try to get into shape for a visit to California. A few weeks after the twins' birth, he and Gladys came to Los Angeles in remarkably good spirits, as if nothing were wrong. His appetite seemed better and he walked confidently with his cane. He'd look forward each day to sitting in a chair between the twins' cribs so he could rock them asleep. But one afternoon during a long walk on our street, he tripped, fell hard, and crashed emotionally.

Back in Philadelphia, Duke's crisis-driven demands on doctors led them to prescribe potent pain medications that slowed his thinking into a reverberation of every disappointment in his life. He said he would do anything to get well. His neurosurgeon offered two drastic measures for pain relief: a cordotomy and implantation of a morphine pump. In a cordotomy, the surgeon opens several bony vertebrae in the upper back and slices into the surface of the spinal cord in order to interrupt one of the pathways for pain. A cut one to two millimeters too deep or high can cause paralysis on that side of the body. The pump, useful for pain control in terminal cancer patients, drips morphine into the spinal fluid via a tiny tube implanted through the back. Painkilling opiate floats directly to docks on neurons in the cord and brain stem with fewer side effects than oral or intramuscular dope; but with constant use the brain becomes narcotized, as ever larger doses are required. Both solutions seemed too dangerous. After talking to my desperate mother the Sunday I learned about Cynthia Waterford's accident, I arranged for his admission into the rehabilitation center at Daniel Freeman. He left Philly having told Gladys this was his last chance to get well.

A rheumatologist, neurosurgeon, orthopedist, psychiatrist, and several therapists tried everything they knew to kill his pain and improve his outlook. Injections into trigger points and physical therapy partially relieved the taut, tender muscles of his neck, shoulder, and back. Learning to use an aluminum walker allowed him to walk without hunching forward or lurching sideways. Duke's constant grimace eased a bit only when Barbara brought the twins to crawl around his hospital room. When she discovered his cache of candy bars under a magazine, he acted like a suitor caught in the arms of another woman. But he drifted into silence, then sleep, each time she tried to engage him in conversation.

Duke's doctors had tried to reduce his pain with treatments that acted at every level of the nervous system's pain-modulating network. Aspirin and the newer nonsteroidal anti-inflammatory analgesics like Naprosyn and Feldene were used to attack at the point of tissue injury where sensory receptors in the muscle, skin, and joint first pick up pain messages. They all helped the acute pain that followed a fall, but could not reduce his aching when he walked and put stress on his muscles and ligaments. Transcutaneous electrical nerve stimulation, in which tiny shocks are sent via a peripheral nerve into the spinal cord in an effort to block incoming pain signals, met with only modest success. And opiate analgesics like codeine and antidepressants like amitriptyline, which activate a natural pathway for inhibiting pain, were limited to doses too small to be effective before they produced side effects.

There was also the problem of Duke's deteriorating concentration and memory. Just what neuronal processes take place to enable learning and memory is still poorly understood. Perhaps the brief electrochemical message passed from one nerve cell to another alters the chemical docks in the synapse. Repeated firing might strengthen this change so it persists indefinitely and becomes the stuff of a memory.

One clear prerequisite for the making and expression of memories is that the neuronal networks in the cortex must be aroused by the thalamus. The cortex, always busy with millions of simultaneous transactions across its synapses, must be alert to sort through what's important and worth retaining. The left brain, which is especially adept at retaining what's heard and read, must be driven by the left thalamus to function efficiently. For instance, PET-scan studies show that when a subject listens to a story with the intention of retelling it later, a small region of the left frontal lobe heats up its metabolism, as if to analyze and help encode signals that arrive first in the portion of the temporal lobe that handles hearing. The reduction in metabolism in Duke's left frontal lobe limited what he could do with such verbal information and impaired this aspect of memory.

By increasing the availability of neurotransmitters to Duke's thalamus and cortex, I hoped to jack up his brain's electrochemical drives. So I tried stimulant drugs like amphetamines and other substances that might increase the amount of several of the over-forty chemical messengers used by neurons. It was a shot into the dark of brain function—and it did not work.

Over Duke's protests about being a burden on Barbara, I enticed him to leave Daniel Freeman on a pass and join us that weekend at home. He smiled and puffed away at his pipe as the twins babbled and splashed in the pool. After his nap, he played with them, then ate everything Barbara cooked for dinner. Over steaming black coffee, his favorite drink, he enthusiastically recounted stories for Barbara of his courtship of Gladys. Rambling across his youth, Duke related with a certain satisfaction some of his humorous experiences when, seasick and smoking his first Camels, a tin first-aid box in hand instead of a rifle, he was a soldier in the forces that invaded North Africa and Sicily. I asked about a famous battle near Algiers. He broke off our conversation after saying that a lot of people died and he had doctored many more who were so maimed that they would have been better off dead.

In the early evening, Duke sat on a kitchen chair as the twins held his legs and pulled themselves to a stand. They hugged him simultaneously, as if on cue, and their grandfather nearly wept. Then, suddenly his eyes turned so sad that Barbara and I felt smothered by the relentlessness of his despair. No psychological force was capable of altering a mood so profoundly; it was as if his thalamic pacemaker had just abruptly stopped driving his cortex.

"I must return to the hospital," he monotoned. "I left some paperwork behind." I pulled the babies away and he rose as if lifted by a derrick. He stared ahead and said, "Can we stop off someplace and pick up some Fleet's enemas and chocolate bars?" We could say nothing. Grasping the walker, he plodded into the bedroom.

I followed after him, but stopped abruptly in the doorway. A few feet into the room, Duke buckled like a wounded cowboy dying in slow motion in a fifties Hollywood Western. Both of his hands clawed feebly toward a bureau for support and his eyes were filled with helpless terror. I grabbed him around the chest, hoisted him by his belt, and pulled him down on the bed. Beached on his back, my father looked at me and said, "I'm not getting well. And I can't live like this."

EIGHT

D R. DOBKIN, IS THAT YOU?"

"Uh, huh."

"This is Mrs. Waterford's night-shift nurse calling from Three South. Dr. Spann said to tell you before you left for the hospital that her temp's still elevated. Did you plan to do the L.P. you discussed?"

"Geez, it's five-thirty in the morning," I grumbled.

"Well, the evening shift said in report he wanted you to be called before . . ."

"I'll tap her. Call Dr. Waterford in an hour and let him know I'll be in her room at seven-thirty."

"Spinal tap on Cynthia?" Barbara asked from the pillow next to me.

"She's been running a fever, around a hundred and three yesterday, and nothing's in her urine or lungs to explain it." I swung around to sit on the side of the bed. "Probably nothing serious, but we wanted to make sure she doesn't have meningitis."

"Oh." She closed her eyes.

Barbara had stopped asking if Cynthia was getting any better. Early on, when I still left open some hope for recovery, we occasionally talked about the tragedy. One weekend evening at dinner, when the subject came up, Jessica did a perfect imitation of the drawn look on Barbara's face. It was an unpracticed sadness that didn't belong on an infant. Rebecca had put down her spoonful of yogurt and tried to copy her sister's lowered brow and pursed lips. Cynthia never came up again in our conversations around the children.

I had to be in court, downtown, in four hours, so I started the already warm August day earlier than my hypothalamus and circadian rhythms instructed.

At Freeman, I found Sandy lying on his side facing his wife in her hospital bed, his arm around her waist. He rose casually from under the quilt Cynthia's grandmother had sent. "I was just telling Cynthia about the lumbar puncture—in case she kinda knows what's going on," he said in greeting. Her right eye involuntarily moved a few degrees toward her nose and her arms pointed stiffly toward her recently manicured toenails.

"Oh. Well, you can stay and help hold her on her side with her knees bent, if you'd like."

"Thanks. She'd like that."

A nurse set the disposable L.P. tray on a narrow table, along with a package of sterile rubber gloves and a soft plastic bottle of dark brown antiseptic. As I turned Cynthia sideways so her back faced toward me, my hands ran over her freshly shaven and oiled legs. The nurse noticed my surprise and mentioned under her breath, "We wanted Mrs. Waterford ladylike, what with all the attention she'd be getting this morning." Sandy thanked her.

I carefully gloved, taped a sterile cloth to her back, and, for Sandy's sake, announced each subsequent step in the ritual. Everything I said, Sandy whispered into Cynthia's ear, adding some gentle phrase like, "This won't hurt" or "We'll be finished in a moment, honey." Cynthia never budged. The fluid did not appear clouded with infection, but the lab's final determination would take an hour.

I stopped off in radiology to check a study. A woman named Nellie Fisher had been admitted yesterday by Hal Silverberg, her internist. She had complained of dizziness for a week, something similar to what had happened to her several years ago when her best friend died; and because her husband had died about a month ago, Silverberg thought she was just depressed. She did walk with her feet separated wider apart than I considered usual, but it was a subtle finding in a woman her age, and I had to convince myself that it might have meaning. Nellie had a breast removed six years ago for cancer. That bit of history plus her gait led me to order a CT scan, just to be thorough.

As I held her films up to the white fluorescent panel, I felt as if someone had kicked me in the belly. A lump of tumor the size of a half-dollar was growing in her right cerebellum. I rechecked the name: Mildred Fisher, my consult. I handed the x-rays to our neuroradiologist, more out of need to check reality than to elicit another opinion.

"Pete," I said, "the lady has the most minimal symptoms and signs for this. And her oncologist examined her a month ago and found nothing suspicious for a metastasis."

"That's what it looks like. Amazing," he said, not appreciating the problems that lay ahead. I suppose that happens to radiologists who spend their days with anonymous films, mere impressions of other doctors' patients.

I studied the film again. "It'll be real risky trying to cut it out."

I left a message for Silverberg and the neurosurgeon and ran up five flights to tell Mrs. Fisher. I felt a perverse exhilaration, a medical-intellectual stimulation that accompanies an unusual case or an extraordinary twist of textbook fate. Doctors love this feeling; it refreshens their sensitivity by getting them away from the banality of most of their cases.

Mrs. Fisher dangled her legs over the side of her bed. She

nibbled at her toast and jelly and sipped a cup of tea, her pinky poised daintily off the white cup. Petite and timorous, Nellie had shown none of the hard edge that might come with being raised in a Colorado mining town before the Depression. I explained the CT–scan findings.

"Dear," she said with a puzzled but not frightened expression, "I've had this dizziness before. I'm inclined to believe Dr. Silverberg when he says it's probably just my nerves again. It can't be my breast."

"I wish it weren't, but it is almost undoubtedly cancer." I couldn't begin to explain why her breast launched a bolus of malignant cells to the one place where the body's immune defenses were unable to attack and destroy them. The brain is a natural preserve in which neurons orchestrate their impulses unpoisoned by the chemical and infectious insults that affect the more injury-prone viscera in chest and abdomen. It's best that way. Our most important organ can't afford to be as vulnerable as the body's hoi-polloi organs. But when the nervous system's sophisticated barrier of interlinked membranes and biochemical surveillance collapses, noxious substances and malignancy can wreck the ordered sanctuary.

"You really think it's the breast thing?"

"Well, I'm as surprised as you about this tumor. I only considered it as a remote possibility. But it's there and maybe we're in time to catch it." We discussed the risks of brain damage, even death, that accompanied an attempt at surgical extraction. If the neurosurgeon got it all, there was a good chance of cure. Radiation alone might not destroy enough of the tumor to prevent it from continuing to grow. I suggested she weigh her choices with Silverberg and the neurosurgeon.

"You won't be doing the surgery?" she asked.

"If I do it, there's a one percent chance you'll survive. If a surgeon operates, there's a ninety-five percent chance of survival."

"Well, you're such a dear, but I'd be inclined to take my chances with your man, if Dr. Silverberg agrees. My husband always said, 'Stick it to the devil.' I don't want this cancer cutting me down piecemeal." She returned to tea and toast. I headed for town, and court.

As I entered the Harbor Freeway on my way into the city, where more people speak Spanish and Asian languages than English, a cloudless cerulean sky overhead transformed, as if by osmosis, into a smoggy gray brown on its distant edges. The stand of tall city buildings towering above white and terracotta stucco homes nearly disappeared in the haze.

I so rarely engage in the real world's bustle outside the hospital and office on a workday that I usually look forward, like a tourist, to mingling in the exotica of city life. But this break was not welcome. I prefer to take care of people, not their lawsuits. I try to avoid serving as an expert witness in medical-legal hassles and dislike dickering with lawyers about medical uncertainties. Forensic neurologists must deal with a logic and truth that simply does not exist in biology and doctoring. In this case, however, an attorney had asked that I take the witness stand for a West Los Angeles hospital he represented, to comment on how an old patient of mine had progressed after his transfer to Daniel Freeman for rehabilitation.

Four years ago, Geoffrey Fairchild had been a tall, blond, forty-year-old prototypic California surfer and beach volleyball player who made a good living as an apartment- and office-building broker. When I first examined him at the community hospital, he'd worn a thick gold neck chain, a Rolex watch, and designer jogging shorts, and referred twice to his new Maserati at his Beverly Hills home. He circumvented questions about his paralysis by repeatedly saying, "I'm doing fine," and almost ignored me as I performed my neurologic exam.

He had no strength or sensation below his nipples and had lost all control of his bowel and bladder. I could not be sure whether his weakness arose from injury to the peripheral nerves in his chest and legs or from damage to his spinal cord at the level of his upper back. Other examiners had faced the same dilemma and were equally uncertain as to what had caused Fairchild's paraplegia, which had begun without warning, then progressed over twenty-four hours.

"You seem pretty well adjusted here," I said. "But I agree with your doctors that after three weeks of this, you're overdue for a more intensive rehabilitation program."

"That's not really necessary. I like this room and, besides, I'm feeling more in my legs." He pointed to his dead legs as if I could appreciate his surge of sensation.

"That's good." Whatever he described meant little as a prognostic sign for recovery. "But you ought to start learning paraplegic techniques. You'll want to protect your skin from pressure sores, transfer in and out of a wheelchair with your arms, and . . ."

"I'll wait till I walk again. No sense learning something I won't need." He reached overhead for the trapeze bar, pulled, and reseated himself more upright. It was becoming clear that neither his internist, orthopedic surgeon, nor neurosurgeon offered him a prognosis. They took a "wait-and-see" attitude. I wondered if they expected me to shake him into reality.

Ten days later, at the urging of friends and other doctors, he arrived for rehab, or more accurately, he settled into a room. Two large fishing-tackle boxes, each with three-by-three-inch compartments, eight across and three deep, filled with hundreds of pills and capsules, accompanied him. He proudly reeled off the names of these vitamins, minerals, nucleic acids, amino acids, antioxidants, cell-membrane stabilizers, and lipoproteins, all guaranteed free of sodium and sugar. Fairchild gobbled them on a regular schedule, a routine established by numerous phone conversations with nonphysician holistic practitioners, based partly on their chemical analysis of his hair and so-called allergy testing of his white blood cells. For meals, he ate only vegetables and soy products. He paid scant attention to the therapy aimed at teaching him to compensate for his profound deficits, but embraced a veritable parade of faith healers, homeopaths, Rolfers, and acupressurists who claimed they would make him well. I had agreed to allow these people massage privileges, so long as Geoff participated in my therapy.

A long tunnel with lighting like a subway station connected the parking lot with the gardens and fountains of the court-house. The quadrangle was quiet compared to the rumble of street traffic. Classical music played on unseen loudspeakers. Above the junipers and magnolia trees, City Hall's terraced pyramid reminded me of an ancient ziggurat for ritualistic ani-mal or human sacrifices.

After watching the proceedings for a few minutes, through a window in the oak doors of the superior court's department 38, I walked inside. Geoff Fairchild sat in a lightweight wheelchair in the aisle at the front of four rows of spectators. A short, thin attorney with premature gray in his beard and a widow's peak gestured emphatically at the ceiling like an evangelist calling upon God, as he interrogated an orthopedic surgeon who had been marginally involved in Fairchild's care before his rehabili-tation. The hospital lawyer spotted me and waved me out of the room.

I sat for an hour under a dreary acoustic-tile ceiling in which every other recessed fluorescent fixture was dark. The marble floors and walls of the long corridors reminded me of the weatherless halls at U.C.L.A. We were moving Larry Oubre from there to Freeman for rehab on Monday. He was alert, off all the anti-edema drugs, although he still couldn't move, feel, or see properly. Yet sometimes he denied any weakness and in-vented a reason for his hospitalization. And when I held his own left hand with its unique gold-rope wedding band in front of his emotionless face, he often said it belonged to me. If I in-structed him to raise the left arm, he'd lift the right. When I confronted him with his error, he feebly reached for his left hand by drumming the fingers of his right hand across his chest, but never looked left with his eyes. He'd be a challenge for the therapists.

Dick Gallagher was a real success story. He had steadily improved from his Guillain-Barré syndrome, although I still had no idea if the bloodletting had contributed to his remarkable gains.

I peeked again through the courtroom door. Inside, the jury shifted uncomfortably in their armchairs. I went over to a bank of pay telephones that smelled of cigarette smoke and called Cynthia Waterford's nurse. The microscopic and chemical studies of her spinal fluid were reported as normal. No infection. Then I phoned the neurosurgeon about Nellie Fisher. He had seen the CT scan and wanted to operate on the presumed cerebellar metastasis immediately.

My secretary gave me a half-dozen messages. Carol Barge's husband called for a refill on her new anticonvulsant medication. He said that Carol had had no seizures since starting it last month. I authorized the drug so long as she returned for necessary blood tests and a follow-up exam. After I made two more calls to patients, the courtroom emptied out. I caught the hospital attorney on his way down the hall.

"Glad you could come, Dr. Dobkin," he said. "We're in recess until this afternoon. Oh, this is the pharmaceutical company's attorney." I missed his name.

"Drug company?" I asked.

"Yes, the manufacturers of the flu vaccine. We'll call you to the witness stand at one-thirty sharp. It'll only take a couple of hours, I hope."

"I've wasted my entire morning," I complained. "And I don't understand why you need me. I have no information about the onset of Fairchild's symptoms, if he's blaming his flu shot. And I haven't heard from him in four years."

"It's just a formality. You're the last witness. Don't worry. We'll get your testimony out of the way. You won't have to return tomorrow." Attorneys have such a sweet way with words.

I ate a sandwich in the company of some city pigeons, then took a seat in the courtroom and read a newspaper until court reconvened and a clerk swore me in.

The jury, trying to stay awake after lunch, was seated to my left. After eliciting what I did for a living, my academic credentials and scientific publications, and generalities about my professional relationship to Fairchild, the hospital attorney asked, "As a board-certified neurologist, what is your opinion about the cause of Geoffrey Fairchild's paraplegia?"

"His early symptoms and signs and lab studies were most suggestive of the Guillain-Barré syndrome," I answered, surprised he was interested in my speculation.

"Did something recognizable cause it?"

"Back then, I believed that the flu vaccination he received two or three weeks before onset might have incited an immunologic reaction that inflamed his peripheral nerves and produced the weakness. That was just after the rash of cases of Guillain-Barré caused by the government's Swine Flu vaccine program, so many doctors associated any vaccine made with a virus or grown in an embryo where foreign proteins get mixed in as a possible cause of the disease."

"Yes." He smiled ambiguously. "We've heard quite a bit of testimony about these vaccines. Do you still believe in this association?"

"Well, the Center for Disease Control did a study in which they found no clear-cut relationship between ordinary flu vaccines and Guillain-Barré."

"So the government study found no relationship except with the extraordinary case of the Swine Flu. Doctor, is it the practice in your community to give a prophylactic flu vaccine to someone Mr. Fairchild's age, a young man in excellent health?"

Was he trying to pass blame onto the internist who recommended the shot? "I don't know the general practice for patients without chronic illnesses. I personally would avoid it, but then I see the rare complications that we associate with them."

Through his next series of questions, I described Fairchild's hospital therapies. "By time of discharge," I concluded, "he was as independent as most young paras."

"Did you expect him to return to work?" asked the lawyer.

The patient's attorney jumped from his chair and called, "Objection! Enough of this leading the witness."

"Your Honor . . . ," began my questioner.

"Sustained," mumbled the judge as he bent over to continue his copious notetaking. Then the hospital lawyer found a way for me to say that paraplegic patients very often returned to their jobs or retrained for work that was sedentary, as long as complications such as skin breakdown and bladder infections were avoided. Was it possible that Fairchild never returned to his real-estate business?

"Doctor, why do you remember Mr. Fairchild?"

"I suppose because he's about my age and suffered a tragic fluke of a nervous-system injury." The lawyer's hesitation urged me further. "Also, he desired more control over his treatment than most patients."

"Really, Doctor? Please tell us, did Mr. Fairchild have a mind healer?" Now I was catching on. The hospital, whatever the basis for its being named in this suit, hoped to show Fairchild as a malingering loon who needed less financial support than he sued for.

Turning to the jury, I said, "He invited a number of non-medical consultants in, who used what I'd consider odd interventions."

"Go on," the attorney urged. Fairchild smoothed the beige blanket over his legs and quickly studied the jury.

"For example," I began, suddenly feeling as if I were gossiping, "a Polynesian group who called themselves holistic healers recommended herbs and enemas, and they used a little gadget to check what they said were his meridians for bodily-energy aberrations. With a lot of fanfare, they'd run something that looked like a voltmeter over his legs and body, and they'd massage an irregular energy area with various perfumed oils. They also burned his thigh with incense when he went out on a weekend pass, which led to a serious bedsore. I think he stopped using this particular group when I ran the meter over a bowl of gelatin and got the needle gauge to deflect the same way it did over his so-called meridians."

The hospital attorney straightened his vest, letting my comments sink into the jury, then asked, "From your experience, would a patient with Mr. Fairchild's degree of impairment require a full-time attendant or extensive vocational rehabilitation?"

Fairchild was asking for damages that would pay for that? "No. I would have thought he'd be independent enough to transact much of his business on the phone and in meetings."

"That's all, Your Honor."

I sipped a glass of water while Fairchild's attorney shuffled his papers and set the stage for his cross-examination.

"Doctor, are you saying Mr. Fairchild had the Guillain-Barré syndrome?" his attorney began, as if reassuring the jury and me of the correctness of the diagnosis.

"More likely than not."

"More likely than not? Do you mean beyond a reasonable medical doubt? Please answer yes or no."

"I believe so." He frowned. "Yes."

"Now, Doctor, do you know a neurologist named George McDonald?"

"Yes."

"He holds a prestigious position in one of the professional societies to which you belong. Is that right?" I nodded. "Please let the court hear your answers."

"Yes."

"Is he a competent neurologist, from your dealings?"

"Certainly."

"Well, sir." The lawyer smiled at the jurors. "He has reviewed the hospital records and testified that Mr. Fairchild suffers from a transverse myelitis, not Guillain-Barré. Would you agree with him?"

"No."

"I see. Could you explain to the jury what a transverse myelitis is?"

"It's more a description of a clinical or pathologic picture than a diagnosis that explains the cause of the victim's problem. A short segment of the spinal cord becomes injured. This blocks most or all the information that passes through the nervous-system pathways at that level. The brain cannot tell the nerve cells in the cord below the block to fire and signal their muscles to move. And the sensory receptors cannot tell the brain about movement or feeling in the skin and limbs below the block. Infections, trauma, a plug in the cord's blood supply, multiple sclerosis, and immunologic diseases can cause it."

"Please explain to those of us less knowledgeable than you why you disagree with Dr. McDonald, a neurologist of some renown."

"From the first examination at the onset of Mr. Fairchild's weakness to the time of discharge from Daniel Freeman, his deep tendon reflexes were absent and he showed no signs of spasticity in his legs. Reflexes are usually brisk within a month or so after a spinal-cord injury, and leg tone is increased—spastic, not flaccid. An injury to the peripheral nerves, as in the Guillain-Barré syndrome, makes the victim *lose* reflexes and tone. The high concentration of protein without any of the white cells that might accompany a spinal-cord inflammation, found in his spinal fluid at the time of the myelogram, the morning after he became paralyzed, and the slowing of his nerve-conduction velocities the next day when his doctors ordered the electromyogram, all fit better with an inflammation of his nerve roots and peripheral nerves than an inflammation at one level of the spinal cord itself. But Mr. Fairchild refused further tests at Freeman to definitively establish the location of his pathology."

The lawyer ignored my logic and asked rhetorically, "So you would disagree with the senior neurologist, Dr. McDonald? Tell me. Does not a sensory level, a clear-cut demarcation of loss of sensation at the upper chest, with paralysis below, point to a spinal-cord lesion?" The attorney slashed his palm across his breast.

"Yes, it can. But, nervous-system diseases don't always go by the book. About three percent of Guillain-Barré patients have such sensory levels, according to a series of one hundred cases published from the University of Michigan in the sixties. And I've had two other cases myself."

"I see." He thumbed through a pile of legal-size yellow sheets and asked offhandedly, still looking down, "Why was Mr. Fairchild's progress in rehabilitation slow?"

"It took him a few weeks to fully participate in our therapies. He had pain problems, his blood pressure dropped enough to make him light-headed whenever he dangled his legs over the bed, and he tended to follow through more on the instructions of his outside consultants than on our recommendations."

"Did you feel he was not motivated?" he asked, looking at the jury.

"Not exactly."

"Well, didn't you write in your initial history and physical that he was? Isn't this your note?" He dropped a copy of the hospital chart on the ledge of the witness stand.

"Yes. But, as it turned out, he refused conventional treatments for those problems. He'd often refuse any medication or take much less than a therapeutic dose."

"Doctor. Didn't you tell Mr. Fairchild that he'd never walk again?"

"As far as I know, I was the only physician who leveled with him and said he'd have to learn to compensate for his sensorimotor loss. I did not know for sure at the time if he would remain paralyzed."

"You leveled with him." His voice filled with contempt. "Doctor, do you believe in faith?"

"You mean faith in general?" I asked limply.

"Yes. Doctor, is it important to have faith?" he repeated like a tent evangelist.

"Well, yes."

"In medicine, is it good to believe in the doctors?"

"Of course. Much of what we do depends on a patient's believing in what we say and giving us and nature a chance to heal."

"And in rehab? Is it any different in rehab?"

"No. People do best when they believe they'll achieve the goals we set, when they're motivated."

"So you depend on motivation, but you gave Mr. Fairchild no hope?"

"Not no hope," I said. "He kept insisting he did not need therapy because his legs would get better on their own. He did nothing for weeks. And his other doctors were unable to admit to him that the paralysis might go on for months or forever. I tried to suggest this to him, but all he got out of our conversations was that I believed he'd never walk."

"Doctor, let me read your note of the twenty-third of March, only the tenth week after onset of Mr. Fairchild's unfortunate paralysis, and thirteen weeks after his vaccination. 'Prognosis for ambulation seems very poor.' You wrote that without being sure of the cause of his paralysis?"

"He resisted having the electromyogram repeated and the bladder tests that might have established the Guillain-Barré diagnosis, as opposed to one of transverse myelitis. I suspected that he feared learning about something that carried a bad prognosis. And I told him the distinction at that point didn't matter. It was academic. The treatment was the same."

"You didn't care about the cause of your patient's illness?"

"My patient needed to have a fire built under him to start learning to compensate," I counterpunched. "Blindly encouraging the belief he'd walk again produced no gains. Even after three weeks of psychological counseling, he did little more than talk on the phone and get his legs stretched and massaged."

"Doctor, how much therapy do patients get a day in your rehabilitation program?"

"The whole day offers various kinds of therapy—physical and occupational therapy, psychosocial intervention, general education about the illness. Even meals and going to the bathroom are learning situations."

"But Mr. Fairchild only received three hours a day of formal treatment the whole first month. Why didn't you provide the usual allocation?"

"He suffered with severe burning in his feet and genitals,

worse with movement, and his blood pressure was extremely unstable when he sat up."

"So you withheld therapy. I see. Couldn't you treat these problems?"

"He wouldn't permit it until the last four weeks of his stay."

"So he really only had four weeks, just one month of optimal therapy before you discharged him?" The lawyer's arguments skimmed and plunged, leaving a wake of implications meant to bias the jury.

"That was all he required to accomplish enough to be independent at home."

"I gather from the record that Mr. Fairchild was in considerable pain. And you ordered codeine?"

"He wouldn't try the nonnarcotic medications that often work, so I left a standing order for that in case he couldn't sleep."

"That's sixty milligrams. Is that a therapeutic dose for such severe pain induced by his disease?"

Was he accusing me of not treating the pain adequately because I wanted to punish the patient? "Given at three- to four-hour intervals, it's a reasonable trial dose."

"Codeine is a narcotic and potentially addicting, I presume?"

The innuendo for the jury was that I tried to turn my patient into a junkie. Or is he reminding them that his client suffered and perhaps still suffers episodic pain requiring financial compensation? "It could be addicting, but the patient only used it a few times in desperation before he allowed me to treat his pain with amitriptyline and Tegretol, two nonaddicting drugs."

The attorney who had dragged me into this, the hospital's lawyer, almost gloated whenever blame diversified toward me and away from his client. Fairchild's attorney must have been trying to prove his client suffered repeatedly from nonchalant, inadequate care that demanded remuneration. In the absence of malpractice, he went after the community hospital's deep pockets. There had been a ruckus, I recalled, about the night-duty nurse not reporting his worsening to his physicians for several hours. Fairchild's workup and treatment would not have differed, but the attorney did have a certain way of distorting events. And he presumably sought retribution from the pharmaceutical company that, he would have argued, did not clearly enough warn of possible rare neurologic complications of its vaccination, such as a transverse myelitis.

"Doctor, from your curriculum vitae, I gather you had been in practice only a short time when you took over my client's care. How many acute paraplegics had you cared for up to then?"

"In rehab, about a dozen similar to Fairchild."

"Just twelve?" he mocked in feigned disbelief and walked within a few feet of the witness stand. "With that amount of experience, were you upset that your patient insisted on having some control over his care?"

"No. As long as he participated in our so-called traditional therapies and did not step beyond the bounds of hospital and medical-legal liabilities, I left him on his own. It was his body and future."

"Surely, doctor, you are not accustomed to sharing your authority with your patients and nonmedical practitioners?"

"Actually, I encourage patients to share responsibility in making medical decisions and probably discuss an unorthodox therapy almost daily with my patients. Neurologists accumulate a lot of patients with incurable weakness, memory impairment, tremors, difficulty walking, pain, and problems my wife tells her friends are worse than anything they might imagine. We've got to be open-minded to any diagnostic tool or treatment that might help. And we've got to be prepared to protect these disabled people from dangerous, unproven, and unscrupulous practices."

"So, Dr. Dobkin, you took a traditional, scientific approach to Geoffrey Fairchild's rehabilitation while he was under your care?"

"Rehab methods are not as well proven as the efficacy of

many drug and surgical procedures for specific diseases. But no one has shown me any better results in patients studied as closely as ours."

"Doctor, please only answer the questions. Did you take the traditional approach with Mr. Fairchild?"

"Yes."

The lawyer's voice grew more shrill. "Then is it true that you hold holistic methods in low esteem?"

I sipped some water and gathered my thoughts. "There are many reasons why I'm suspicious of so-called holistic preachings." Leaning toward the jury, the only people in that courtroom for whom I felt any responsibility on this issue, I said, "They're an unregulated and almost always untested, mixed bag of common sense and ancient and occult methods generally not applied with their original intent. Makeshift answers do not warrant the title of a system of thought or healing. The people who claim to be holists are not trained in any basic fund of knowledge. Their commonality, at least as I see the spectrum of practice in Southern California, is a belief in preventive health care and being responsible for your own mental and physical well-being. I believe in that, too, and make suggestions to patients that might come from the mouth of any thoughtful health-foods addict, acupuncturist, herbalist, chiropractor, Feldenkrais, or Rolfer. And so does even the most conservative of physicians."

"Then perhaps there are economic reasons . . ."

"Excuse me, I'm not finished. I won't get into the complete lack of evidence that examining the iris or tongue allows a diagnosis of organic disease, or the complete lack of reproducibility in exposing white blood cells to so-called allergens to find out what substances make a person sick, or the failure to show efficacy of cracking a back to heal an internal organ and dieting to cure cancer. My greatest concern about what I perceive to be a fundamental tenet of this enthusiastic, almost religious amalgam of self-proclaimed alternative therapists is that they say or imply that people are *responsible* for their own unwellness. It is trite to say that no disease would exist if we were all in perfect harmony with our bodies and spirits. What does that mean? But the assertion breeds guilt in the believer. His sickness becomes some self-imposed retribution. Maybe, he imagines, his legs become paralyzed because he spent forty years eating the wrong foods and unleashing his Type A personality."

Hands gripping the back of his chair, eyes searching the neat piles of notes on his table, the attorney asked, "Doctor, is Mr. Fairchild still in pain?"

"I have not seen or heard about him since a few weeks after his rehab discharge. He chose to make his own arrangements for outpatient care."

"Of course. You didn't follow up in your care of your patient. That's all, Your Honor."

His contempt stunned me into angry stillness. And he was seated and whispering to a colleague before I could counter his abusive misrepresentation. Again, the hospital lawyer let me fry. I turned to the robed judge. He puckered his lips, peered over his reading glasses, and said only, "You may step down."

NINE

W ATCH OUT FOR RAUL COMPOS," called Helena, the head nurse on the Two Northeast wing of the rehabilitation center. I was standing in front of the activities board that tracks the daily schedule of therapies for each of the twenty-five patients on the stroke ward and was about to begin my rounds. Helena grinned. "His wife's about to canonize you."

Mrs. Compos and her sister-in-law stood at either side of Raul's bed looking like two schoolgirls with a secret. Mrs. Compos proclaimed, "Here comes that Dr. Dobkin," and her husband sat as upright as he could. He wore brown slacks belted so high above his waist that only his top three shirt buttons showed. A year ago, Raul had weighed forty pounds more.

"Everything going okay?" I asked the group.

"Oh, it's just a miracle how well he's doing." Mrs. Compos glowed. "We prayed for this. He's so much more there. I mean, he feeds himself, rolls over in bed, and sits by himself. And would you believe he walked ten steps into the bathroom with that wonderful therapist Susan?"

Raul said, "Doc, I'm thinking about going home. You get me outta here in one piece and I'll prune those white and scarlet oleanders around the doctors' lot. Gotta cut 'em back or they'll have nothing but green leaves and stalks next year."

A change in what blooms in Los Angeles marks the seasons before there's a shift in the weather. The oleander blossoms near the lot had begun to brown and curl like parchment, declaring the end of summer. It was the first time in a year that Raul had noticed the change in the seasons.

"All that time, why didn't other doctors see his problem?" Mrs. Compos asked, patting a trace of chocolate pudding from Raul's chin.

I rotated Raul's arms back and forth to test for residual stiffness. "The symptoms creep up on the patient and his doctor and sometimes are mistaken for some natural aspect of aging. When Raul had his stroke, no one paid further attention to why he never really improved, even though some of his strength returned. These things happen."

Nine weeks ago, an ambulance service wheeled Mr. Compos by gurney into my office examining room. He was unable to speak intelligibly, so Mrs. Compos provided his history. Ten months earlier, he suffered an acute paralysis of his left face, arm, and leg and lost his swallowing reflexes. After clearing up a bout of pneumonia caused by inhaling his saliva, his doctor put a nasogastric tube in him for liquid feedings and shipped him off to a nursing home, telling his wife there was little hope of any recovery. Mrs. Compos practically moved into the nursing home with Raul. She encouraged him to swallow again and got the staff to lift him into a chair. When Raul learned to swallow pureed foods without choking, she brought him to me.

"I'll do anything to have him home again," she had told me. "Can't afford full-time help in the house, and besides, we've only got a one-bedroom apartment, so no one could live in anyway. But if he could just help himself enough to get from bed into a wheelchair and walk maybe ten feet into the bathroom, I know I could manage, even with my back and heart situation." She was short and heavy, with the curved, knobby fingers of an osteoarthritic, and she was unrealistic. Her husband had trouble walking for at least a year before his stroke and now had been bed-bound for months. How could she expect me to get him walking? But my exam made me reconsider her fantasy.

In the office, Compos was able to elevate his arm and leg a few inches off his gurney, though his hand and foot muscles only twitched. Sensation, vision, and cognition were surprisingly normal for an eighty-one-year-old supposedly so disabled that he had been committed to a nursing home. His weakness was best explained by the plugging of a tiny artery that had fed a deep patch of white matter in his right hemisphere called the internal capsule. This dime-size patch is an anatomical funnel for movement commands coming down from the motor cortex on their way to the brain stem and spinal cord. Nearly all our rehab patients with capsular infarcts return home able to walk. Raul had failed to make any progress toward mobility before coming to Freeman because he suffered with another underlying neurologic disease.

His arms and legs flexed and extended with ratchety rigidity as if his joints were attached to a stiffly rotating cogwheel. Lying on the gurney, his head, neck, and shoulders arched forward as if he were about to sit up but had frozen, sapped of all vitality. His face showed no spontaneous expression; it was like a mask sculpted in a pale, blank stare.

"What was his walking like before the stroke?" I asked.

"Not that bad. His feet hurt all the time, so he was kinda slow."

"What do you mean by slow?"

"Well, over a year ago when I took him to the doctor's, he nearly got trampled when people behind us in an elevator came out a lot faster than Raul could get going. At home, he was mostly stuck in a chair, watching TV."

"Did he take short steps?" I pursued. She sighed as if trying to describe some characteristic that had never before seemed abnormal, but suddenly took on new meaning. "See if this helps. Did he walk at all like this?"

I hastily shuffled in half-foot steps like an automaton driven from behind, lurching slightly forward with arms glued at my sides as if I were wearing an inflexibly starched shirt. "Yes," Mrs. Compos cried out, sensing we were on to something. "That's what happened more and more, especially when he first stood up to walk."

In 1817, a modestly successful London general practitioner had detailed Raul's symptoms without having any notion as to what caused them. His "Essay on the Shaking Palsy" described the soft monotone voice, stiff and hypokinetic face and body movements, muscle rigidity, and involuntarily short, marching steps that Raul's wife recalled. The hallmark feature of the disease is a tremor of the hands that looks as if the patient were rolling a pencil between the thumb and fingers. But in Raul's case, it was not present. The author, under the pseudonym "Old Hubert," also wrote pamphlets with titles like "Revolutions without Blood," and barely escaped British imprisonment for his political views. As a dilettante paleontologist, he developed theories of evolution in a three-volume illustrated work on the shells and formations of the Dover cliffs, called *Organic Remains of a Former World.* But his name has been memorialized for what neurologists later designated as Parkinson's disease.

I admitted Raul to the rehab ward on a trial basis. After ten days of intensive physical therapy and the medication Sinemet, he began to escape the dopamine-deficient cocoon that had created his symptoms before his stroke and worsened them from inactivity after it. His emergence from stiffness and rigidity to flowing and spontaneous movements was a miracle even to me, though I understood its physiologic basis.

In Parkinson's disease, the neurons in the upper brain stem that make up a darkly pigmented tissue called the substantia nigra begin to slowly die out. These nigral cells ordinarily release a chemical neurotransmitter called dopamine from the tips of their axons. The dopamine messenger then floats across the tiny gaps, or synapses, between the nigral cells and the neurons of the basal ganglia and stimulates them to pulse messages to yet other neurons. One loop of this system simply feeds back to the substantia nigra. Another leads to the thalamus, which, along with information it gets from the cerebellum, regulates movements.

Each clump or network of neurons along these circuits is ultimately linked directly or indirectly with nearly every other area of the brain, because it may take, depending on what's going on in a person's mind and environment, almost any other brain function, whether memory, emotion, vision, perception, or whatever, to help influence a smooth, rapid, and precise movement. When so many nigral cells die that they are no longer able to release enough dopamine for the nigral-to-basal ganglia loop, a disconnection takes place that causes some of the components of movement to break down. We treat the Parkinson's victim with a medication containing L-dopa, which the brain converts into the neurotransmitter dopamine, allowing the patient to regain at least some of the efficient, smooth grace with which he once moved.

Why nigral cells degenerate in some people is unclear. In the case of people who survived the flu pandemic around 1918, it seems likely that a virus might have been the culprit. Years later, they developed typical Parkinson's symptoms. Autopsies in this group revealed a profound loss of nigral cells. In 1978, a street drug-user developed typical symptoms and signs of Parkinson's from the by-product, called MPTP, of a narcotic he had synthesized in his illicit basement laboratory. When he died from a drug overdose, researchers found nigral-cell degeneration identical to classical Parkinson's. This drug-induced Parkinson's has also been experimentally reproduced in monkeys. The implication that viruses and toxic chemicals can destroy particular sets of neurons raises new and profound insights into many neurologic diseases, especially those involved with psychiatric and memory disorders. If you add the small percentage of brain cells that die with normal aging to those destroyed by exposure to a virus or environmental toxin, you might cross the threshold into still-mysterious illnesses like ALS and Alzheimer's dementia.

"We was sure, wasn't we, Alma," said the sister, "that Raul's brain was goin' to pot?"

"I was real uneasy all those months in the nursing home. Even before the stroke." Mrs. Compos confided to me, "I watch over him real careful 'cause he's such a good husband." Raul's eyes moistened as she massaged the weak left hand.

"He's on rehab because of your persistence," I said. "We plan a discharge next Wednesday with all the equipment and continuing outpatient therapy you'll need."

"Will you be our doctor?" Raul asked with new strength and melody in his voice. I nodded.

"Good," said the wife. "Poor Nellie Fisher—she's our neighbor, you know—lost her doc." Mrs. Fisher had come through her tumor surgery without a hitch and returned home a week later. The mass was a breast metastasis that shelled out from normal surrounding cerebellum like a pit from a peach, curing her at least for a time.

"Dr. Silverberg just died?" I asked. He had discussed a case with me two days ago.

"No, he retired. But she cries the same. She's been going to him since the days of three-dollar office visits. Sent his kids birthday presents until they married. They don't make doctors like him no more. You know what a mensch is?" asked this third-generation Mexican-American. "That's him. Always there for you."

Silverberg was only in his early sixties, but the paperwork and business end of solo medical practice had grown overwhelming for him. He told me a year ago that he wanted to get out of medicine before he woke up one morning and found himself working for a Health Maintenance Organization, government Medicare program, or corporate health-care giant that set, for him, intolerable bureaucratic and financial limits on how to treat his patients.

Before I left, Mrs. Compos handed me a carrot cake and two stuffed bunnies for my kids.

Another physician almost certain to be forced into retirement was being wheeled by his wife down the hall in a commode chair. In his fourth week on the rehab unit, Larry Oubre so feared his occasional incontinence of bowels and bladder that he preferred traveling on the hard plastic donut seat with a pan underneath rather than a padded wheelchair. I followed him into a room overflowing with sympathy cards, sprawling green and ivory pothos, broad fiddleleaf fig leaves, and bright seasonal flowers. Someone had shaved clean his mustache. His hair had grayed at the sideburns.

Mrs. Oubre crimped her lips as Larry pulled his left forearm through his shoulder sling with the right hand. "We're so glad to be here. Larry's really starting to make progress."

"He has improved," I agreed. A few weeks ago, Oubre couldn't keep his head upright or sit in a chair without slumping down to his left. "With the insight the left side of his brain has started to gain, I think we can get him standing and handling his own wheelchair in another two weeks. And maybe he'll be walking with a cane and ankle brace in another month or two."

Larry's therapists had been working with him to get his left shoulder, hip, and knee to move by stimulating complex brainstem and spinal-cord reflexes. We vibrated over tendons, compressed his large joints, and placed air splints on his left knee to help the joint bear his weight. Larry also spent a lot of time rolling on an exercise mat from his back to his side in order to coax the weak leg to bend reflexively.

Physical therapies are as much witchcraft as applied neurophysiology. Since Larry's right cortex and basal ganglia had been decimated by his stroke, we were trying to get the rest of his nervous system to compensate and re-establish some control over his left limbs. What stimuli we put in and what responses came out no longer followed ordinary anatomic pathways. The neurons in the brain stem and spinal cord are, evolutionarily speaking, very ancient. They include gross-movement generators that are found in animals who never developed the enormous cerebral hemispheres found in man. Although these generators cannot initiate and coordinate movement in the fine and powerful way that the basal ganglia, cerebellum, and thalamus do in concert with the cortex, they might allow Larry to stand up and walk with effort, despite his loss of strength.

Larry tilted his head to his left shoulder and spoke barely above a hoarse whisper: "Maybe I can make the winter AMA convention."

"Honey, let's worry . . ."

"That's a fair goal," I half lied. He needed a marker in time, an expectation rooted in the world outside the tricks his brain played on him. Larry's eyes were still as vacant as keyholes. The neglect he had shown for his left side in the first days off the respirator at U.C.L.A. had diminished, but at Daniel Freeman, it evolved into a kind of embarrassing inattention. While Dr. Oubre and his wife dealt admirably with the uncertainties and sometimes infantile dependency of his physical paralysis, they had only begun to struggle with the fragmentation of his mind.

The nervous system, of course, is not an undulating digestive tract that breaks down and evacuates intelligence. The brain stores and manipulates vast quantities of constantly changing information which continually moves from one network of neurons to another. This is what creates the complex behaviors we call learning, language, perception, emotion, and thought.

Since Vesalius drew the first anatomically correct sketches of the brain's surface in 1543, neuroscientists have been obsessed with the challenge of mapping the nervous system. Like mariners and geographers, European anatomists explored and named the furrows and elevations of cortical topography. The invention of the microscope in the 1600s led to the discovery of brain cells. But it wasn't until the late 1800s, when scientists were able to selectively color individual neurons and their supporting glial cells, that the brain's cartographers began to study the connections these cells made among themselves. Mapmaking reached one of its peaks in 1909 when an anatomist named Brodmann subdivided the cortex into forty-seven patches, each corresponding to a particular arrangement of neurons that were presumed to serve different purposes in the brain's functions.

There were minor setbacks in the early pursuits of a functional brain map. Speculations about the bumps and grooves of the cortex created the "science" and parlor game of phrenology. Experts believed that the palpable bumps of their clients' skulls reflected the brain's underlying infolds and outpouches—each of which, in turn, was misinterpreted as a trait of character.

Since then, researchers have created maps of cortical function in many ways. First, they electrically stimulated tiny areas of the brain in animals and awake neurosurgical patients and observed what their subjects moved, spoke, or felt. Using the techniques of both modern neurochemistry and the PET scan, researchers have been able to create glowing maps of the pathways between patches of cells as they interact with one another over wide areas of the brain.

Brain maps are like those thick Thomas Brothers street atlases that allow you to look up an address by its page number and by its location at the intersection of a horizontal and vertical axis. In three dimensions, each page might represent a cubic millimeter of the axonal highways that surround a neighborhood of one hundred thousand neuronal businesses, each with an average of five thousand connections with other cells.

In the most developed neighborhoods, many paths reach any destination. Some streets run only a short distance within a page, others course across many pages. The short ones serve local traffic, the long ones tie neighborhood to neighborhood, just as long axons interconnect lobes and hemispheres. Whatever the origin and destination of the streets, traffic tends to move in either direction. Most functionally related neighborhoods of neurons that stimulate another near or distant group will be excited, inhibited, or modulated via a return path from that group. Such feedback fine tunes their cooperative efforts.

Cargo-carrying traffic, the brain's electrochemical messengers, travels the roads on any page of the map, limited only by how fast pedestrians and vehicles can move. Traffic can converge, diverge, and move along parallel routes on its way along chosen paths. Of course, the longer the road, the greater the chance that some natural disaster will make it impassable. When roadblocks threaten the smooth flow of commerce, new routes can sometimes be found and used.

It's the dynamic physiology of the brain, like the commerce of a growing society, that alters routes. Just as government will decide on the need for and the location of roads, our genes wire potentially useful connections between cells so that they can enhance commerce, and ensure survival. Next year's edition of the map will reflect changes in routes. They'll lengthen and widen; a route that has become increasing useful may evolve from a dirt road to a paved primary road to a two-lane highway, and finally to a freeway. When a group of neurons is stimulated to rehearse together time and again, they will create larger and more efficient pathways; this is called learning.

Neighborhoods of neurons are always in flux. Messages stop and go when cells are inhibited and excited, merge along busy lanes, and head out both familiar and little-used roads as they integrate thinking and exert more precise control over the body. Whatever influences one of the interlocked communities may also influence the whole society of cells. Vast repertoires of thought and behavior arise.

The left and right hemispheres hold somewhat separate inventories of knowledge and make separate inferences about the world. The right brain works more from an inductive and holistic point of view, while the left takes a more analytic, less unitary approach and uses more abstract and sequential reasoning. This means that the right tends to handle tasks that involve body image, spatial orientation, and how we perceive what we touch, see, and hear. It does not learn from prior errors as well as the more deductively analytic left brain, which handles symbolic tasks like mathematics and language.

Each hemisphere develops strategies to determine what is

truth and what is error. Via the abundant bridges of the central corpus callosum, the two hemispheres feed each other their concepts at a stage of physiologic information-processing that we still don't understand. PET–scan studies even show that as a music lover becomes expert in understanding the elements of music, he will shift his analysis from his right to his left hemisphere.

If the corpus callosum is split surgically, as it is, sometimes, in order to control the spread of otherwise untreatable epileptic electrical discharges, the messages of one side of the body can then only get in and out of the hemisphere that controls them. The other side of the split brain knows about none of this, since it is now excluded from the conscious experience of its other half. If a split-brain patient is shown, under laboratory testing conditions, the photograph of a composite face that is half-male on the right and half-female on the left, the left cortex sees only a male and the right only a female. If asked to state the sex of the person in the photo, the patient says it's a male, because only the left brain can respond verbally and therefore it dominates. If the right hemisphere were given its chance to respond, by the patient being asked to point to a matching male or female face, the patient would choose, nonverbally, the female.

When a cerebral injury like a stroke destroys any portion of a hemisphere, each side of the brain deals with new circumstances based on old or incomplete information. The plethora of symptoms that the neurologist finds in people with brain injuries reflects the disconnection of the integration and interdependence of the hemispheres and the widespread networks of neurons within each hemisphere. So while a localized brain injury often measurably impairs some sensory, motor, or cognitive function, the lesion may cause broader, less obvious consequences as well.

But this interdependency has a positive side to it. It's possible that the genetically determined, intricate weave of cerebral roadways within and between hemispheres evolved precisely in order to enhance the chances for survival in case of a relatively minor cerebral injury. The vast and sometimes redundant connections between neurons mean that the brain can sometimes compensate for one roadblock by using an uncommon pathway or far-flung strategy.

One of our first tasks with Larry Oubre had been to get him to stop neglecting everything that happened on his left side. The parts of the neuronal network that ordinarily interact when we pay attention to the environment include the brain stem's reticular activating system (which stimulates arousal and vigilance); the parietal lobe (which helps organize spatial information); the temporal lobe (which motivates attentiveness and links up memory); and the frontal lobe (which handles the programs for initiating and carrying out movement). Larry's stroke destroyed most if not all of these interlocked pathways on the right side of his brain, so we had to arouse his left hemisphere.

We instructed Larry not to begin to read, write, or eat until he located a vertical red band we'd placed at the left side of his book, or margin of his paper, or edge of his table. This anchor was his starting marker. Getting him to compensate when he was in motion was harder and a little dangerous. At first, he'd propel his wheelchair in right-handed circles and smash into people and door frames. But in the past week, he had finally begun to dredge up an analysis by his left brain, which helped him to gradually shift the midline of his world from someplace off to the right to nearer the center of whatever he looked at.

"Think I'll get anything back in my left hand?" Larry asked in a flatly metered tone, as if not interested in my answer. But he was. None of the prosody that, more subtle than words, conveys the anger, concern, and humor of communication had returned to his speech. And he couldn't grasp the emotions in the voices or faces of those around him. It was another lost right-brain function.

"It'll take a while longer to see how the hand will do. The right hand's the noble one anyway, the one that speaks for kings and popes. We'll continue concentrating on your balance and mobility. That's what you need to get home."

"And back to work?" he asked.

A rehabilitation center is a sanctuary where the physically and emotionally paralyzed are helped to break the link between their unexpected illness and their fear of dying. They are asked to give more energy and desire than they've ever before devoted to a task, in order to make the best of their survival. Cures are rare in people whose stroke, head trauma, or spinal-cord injury are devastating enough to require inpatient rehab. Our aim is to improve the quality of patient life, emphasizing the skills that will give them the independence to return home. By necessity, rehabilitation promotes a patient's acceptance of his condition.

"Hi, sweetheart," Mrs. Copland called from her wheelchair. "Oops, guess I should call you 'doctor.'" The sixty-year-old Mrs. Copland had been an actress in what she described as a pleasant, if undistinguished career.

"You can call me anything you want as long as you keep pushing yourself in gait training. So what's up? Did you give the medical residents I sent a hard time?"

"I was good. When this kid, couldn't be over twenty-five, says, 'Now I don't want you to take this the wrong way, Miz Copland, but could you tell me the name of the president?' I almost died. I was going to tell her Coolidge but figured that would destroy the little thing."

"Medical education thanks you. How's your roommate?"

She bowed her head and threw up her left arm. "She just lies there staring, she moans whenever a therapist moves her, and the family hovers and worries. Gets me down. The poor thing spits out the food her own daughter feeds her."

"She'll come around. I'm working on it. You're moving your fingers a little more."

"Yeah, but it still feels like I'm holding a dead canary. What's really been bugging me is that people come and visit me and have nothing to say." She scowled broadly enough to transmit her disdain to the back rows of a theater. "I mean, they tell you how good you're doing and how well you look—and under their breaths they go, 'Thank God it isn't me.' I swear, even old friends come to purify themselves and see what they can do to not become me."

I shrugged my shoulders sympathetically. She hit on something I had begun to sense in myself. The night I admitted Cynthia Waterford, I got home hours after Barbara had gone to bed. I lay down beside her and suddenly felt overwhelmed by that past week—Cynthia and Sandy, the Oubres and the Gallaghers, Duke and my family in Philadelphia. It was all too close and too sad. I touched the back of my hand to Barbara's cheek and held back the pain and fear in the moment it was meant to pour out. After a while, I could sleep.

In the dining room, sitting under color photographs of pink and yellow hibiscus, two aphasic patients—people who had suffered a loss of their comprehension and/or expression of speech—ate lunch with their left hands.

"Mr. Chui, is the shoulder any better?" He had developed a mild biceps tendonitis from overstretch of the paralyzed right arm. As I pressed over the tendon and rotated the slightly spastic limb, his face belied no discomfort.

He scrutinized me and made the sound "eeeooo." Then he shook his head and tried again: "eeyo." His frustration mounted. Out of the forty-five or so basic sounds in English, Mr. Chui could pronounce only a few. Six weeks earlier, a blood clot not much wider than a pencil eraser formed in a damaged heart chamber after a moderately severe heart attack, broke free, and traveled to his brain, where it plugged a major cerebral artery. The area of the frontal lobe that helps control speech, Broca's region, bore the brunt of the stroke and disconnected Mr. Chui's speech and writing machinery from other language areas vital to comprehension. His therapist was able to get him to utter two to three word phrases by teaching him to hum a few bars of a melody and then intone words to the melody. This method presumably provided the patient with a different, though much less efficient, pathway than the one the stroke disconnected and gave Chui at least some access to his underlying knowledge of words. It was also possible that the right side of his brain had some rudimentary vocabulary that the musical technique brought to life. Over the next four months, he'd likely learn to speak a handful of short phrases and convey meaning with head nods and face and hand gestures.

His dining partner smiled at me. "Are you getting better, Mrs. Altomare?"

"Thinka," the grandmotherly woman replied.

"What did you do today?"

"How can I . . . I did marts stan. I worked at . . . the man . . . he was . . . we did little tacks. From here. The little therple fixed people. . . . This isa terble." She laughed.

"Take your time."

She smiled again sheepishly. "I ah had it before but not doing it. I know there's something but I'm not getting."

"You worked in therapy?" I offered. "On the mats with the therapists?"

"Yes! I say it do it. I know it's there. I did that, doing this."

She could not repeat phrases or name objects we gave her without responding with jargon that often substituted nonsense words and sounds for what she wished to say. But she was improving. She used body language to compensate for what her sometimes contentless speech failed to convey. Even though the left brain houses the bulk of language skills, an injury there that produces aphasia still permits the rich innuendo of meaning and emotion that's contained in facial gestures and variations in the pitch and tempo of even limited speech. An example of this is found in those stroke victims who, otherwise speechless, are able to be quite fluent with profanities that convey their frustration.

In a nearby room, I found Nobe Tanaka's wife applying dabs of what smelled like wintergreen balm, from the base of his left thumb up his arm to his shoulder. Then she covered each pearly dab with a square of white adhesive tape. This patient's stroke was as severe as Larry Oubre's, but had resulted from a massive hemorrhage in his right hemisphere caused by poorly controlled hypertension.

"Dr. Dobkin, so glad to see you," she enunciated in the Japanese-American accent in which the tongue slaps sound between the palate and closed teeth. "I use this old remedy on my husband for the pain he has."

"I didn't realize he was having any pain." His left arm and leg were paralyzed and felt nothing. And he still ignored his environment on the left side. Some cerebral swelling from the bloody mass persisted and disrupted in subtle ways the alertness of even the left cerebrum. "Mr. Tanaka, does the arm hurt anyplace in particular?"

He mumbled dispassionately and barely intelligibly, "Detectives here take arm to factory."

"Detectives?"

Mrs. Tanaka clarified: "He thinks they take his body to detention camp. Like when we lived here during war. When he goes for x-ray yesterday, he thinks they're locking him up."

His delusion sounded more bizarre than anything Larry Oubre expressed. I held Tanaka's left arm in his right visual field. "What is this?" I asked.

"Arm."

"Whose arm?"

"My hand."

"Yes." I gently squeezed his right biceps. "It is your left arm and hand, the one paralyzed by your stroke. No harm can come to it or to you. You're here for therapy that will help it work again."

"Yes. I do therapy."

The wife's teeth showed in a grimacing smile.

"Mrs. Tanaka. Try to correct his misconceptions as you hear them. His brain's still playing tricks on him."

"I do that." She held up a plastic bag of persimmons and

said, "This for you. You like? Please take." I could not refuse, even if my brown-canvas attaché began to look more like a shopper's than a doctor's. I added the fruit to Mrs. Compos's bunnies and carrot cake.

Dick Gallagher and I collided as I left Tanaka's room. He grabbed my shoulder to steady himself. His arms and legs had thinned, but in his navy rugby shorts and striped T-shirt, he looked fit and strong.

"Hey, I'm sorry," he said. "Didn't mean to bite the hand that heals me."

"It must be time to get you out of here."

The ebullient physical therapist at Dick's side protested that she wanted to work more on walking outdoors on uneven surfaces. Therapists become so devoted to their patients that they hate to lose those who do well and those who might improve further with intensive inpatient care. But it costs too much—up to six hundred dollars a day—to continue inpatient therapy on someone who can make effective, if slower, gains as an outpatient. Discharge is often a time of anguish. It's the rare patient and family who feel ready to break the umbilical link to the rehab team. The patient wants his weak hand to grasp better, his therapist wants his gait smoother, and families find the victim's halting steps, ungainly postures, and speech or perceptual problems too disquieting. But the goal of the game is to get the patient home reasonably safe with supervision. Dick did not resist.

"When can I go?" he asked.

"I thought you'd need until next week, but you're good enough to leave Saturday. Just don't overexert yourself."

"Great. I was gonna ask you for conjugal privileges if I had to wait any longer. What about work?"

"I'll see you in the office and we'll decide." His strength had improved enormously, and even the numbness in his hands and feet had resolved.

"I can't believe it." He inspected his palms through tears like those he cried the second night of his admission. I put my hand on his shoulder. "Those first nights, I was so afraid I'd die. My wife and kids ... would they be okay? Before the plasmapheresis, I decided they would. But permanent paralysis. I thought about all those people I've seen in wheelchairs. A friend of ours has a brother who's a quad from a neck fracture. Dived into a shallow pond. I felt so close to people like him, but never believed I could be as courageous as them."

"You did fine. You had it made a week ago," I said, smiling, "but I know how long it takes a rock climber to see handwriting on a wall. When are you going to take your wife out dancing?"

He laughed. "I promised that, didn't I? But I never told her."

"I'll tell her."

"I'll do it. By the way. How's your dad? We talked once or twice a coupla weeks ago over candy bars and coffee just before he left."

I felt instantly depressed, but said, "He's doing okay, as long as he remembers to use his walker. He insisted on going back to Philadelphia. At least he can get out of the house and has less neck pain."

"Send him my regards. He was a big hit here. The doctor's father and all."

A white figure swaddled in towels from head to toe, like a baby fresh from a bath, rotated his wheelchair a quarter turn with his left hand on the wheel and his left heel clawing the green carpet and called, "Hey, Doc. I've got to have a talk with you."

It was Maurice Sawyer, an eighty-year-old tailor who had been living alone in his West Hollywood apartment before his stroke. For the first ten days following his transfer to Freeman, he refused to work at all in therapy. "Leave an old man alone," he'd groan whenever an eager therapist approached. I wanted him to return home walking so we wouldn't have to send him to a nursing home. But after several talks in which he complained without real cause about the food, his roommate, and the demeaning way he felt the "youngsters" on his rehab team spoke to him, and then paid only lip service to participating, I had begun to wonder if it was selfishly wrong to continue trying to shake him into staying alive.

Maurice's neurologic problems were serious. He had a mild aphasia. His right leg was so weak that I empathized with his belief that it would never hold him up again. And, most annoying to a fellow who had made his living with his hands, Sawyer had lost much of his ability to use either hand to carry out the kinds of skilled movements that ordinarily required no thought. Although patients with similar problems had returned home, I could not convince the tailor that anything but total incapacity and death awaited him.

I had almost summarily discharged him, but as I started to write the order in his chart, I realized that the anger and frustration he aroused in me with his petty complaints and his refusal to cling to any hope were really a reaction I carried over from Duke's stay on the ward. So I held off Medicare hospitalization reviewers, who wanted him out because of his lack of progress, and tried to stack the cards in my favor by starting an antidepressant medication and assigning him to the oldest-looking therapists in our stable. Then I invited a former patient his age to talk about how her hard work paid off in her return home. Within a week, his participation improved. We'd soon be able to send him home with a daytime attendant. Now he smiled when he complained.

"Doc," he began with a slow, telegraphic delivery, "I never thought you'd get here. Those woman, ah, I mean nurses, won't let me shower before breakfast."

"Don't they bathe you before you start the day's therapies?"

"Need it before breakfast."

"Why?" I smiled.

"Come on, Doc. You can't get wet right after you eat."

"Sorry, I didn't know that."

"Well, it is, ah, something you know." He winced in his struggle for the word he wanted. "Ah, common sense. Yes."

"You're talking about swimming just after you eat. The digestive tract steals blood from your muscles, so if you use them they might cramp. At least that's what my grandmother told me."

"Well, she might be right. But I been showering, er, things . . . before breakfast. And no changing now."

"Okay. I'll take care of it. By the way, you're expressing yourself much better." He shrugged his shoulders. "Show me how you would lock a door if you were holding a key." He looked at his nearly paralyzed right hand and barely opened it. "Show me with your left hand." He opened and closed the left fist. "Watch how I pretend to turn the key, then you do it." I pinched my thumb and first two fingers together, extended my arm, and turned it a few degrees clockwise. He stuck out a finger and wiggled it.

I held up my keychain. "What are these?" I asked.

"Keys."

"What do you do with them?"

"Open doors and turn on your things."

"Take a key and show me how you'd use it." He thought for a moment, frowned, then buried the keys in his left hand. I demonstrated what I wanted, but he still could not correctly mimic this simple act that he had performed thousands of times without a thought before his stroke. Shortly after his admission, he could name a comb, wash rag, safety razor, and belt, but seemed to have no idea how to use them. His problem, called apraxia, had improved slowly with therapy and he now used those objects properly.

By CT scan, Sawyer's stroke appeared as a small dark hole deep in his left frontal lobe. It damaged the axons that tell the right arm and leg to move and, most remarkably, blocked the road that memories for skillful actions must take when they are called upon to leave their home in the left hemisphere and travel across the corpus callosum to the right brain. If they don't get there, the left hand looks foolish, even though its strength, feeling, and coordination are quite normal. The hand's blueprint for action was missing. Sawyer's neurologic problems were not as much the consequence of losing what any

one group of neurons controlled as they were of losing the connections between the complex subtasks that make up an action.

"You're coming along much faster than I had expected," I
said. "Try not to let the trouble using things get you down."

"How about a back massage?" he asked.

"Anything you can get the nurses to do," I said as I back-
pedaled down the hall and quickly turned the corner.

I reviewed a few more cases with the therapists as they
worked with their patients in the rehab gym, then felt the urge
to check on Cynthia Waterford. The head-trauma service on
another wing of the center was starting her on a trial of stimulation techniques. While Sandy, early every morning and late
each evening, caressed his wife and whispered for up to an hour
in her ears, the therapists used sound, light, smell, vibration,
rocking, and rolling to provide sensory overstimulation. The
input, rhythmical or irregular, might in theory awaken isolated
sensorimotor neurons.

Cynthia stared walleyed at a mirror ten feet in front of her.
Both of her eyes moved horizontally now, but out of synch. Everyone had done a great job preventing the complications of
prolonged immobility. Her eyes were moist and clear, her skin
showed no reddening pressure points or breakdown, and her
joints were loosely mobile. She never ran a fever after my spinal
tap. She took no medications. We fed her liquids through a
tube placed directly through the abdominal wall into her stomach and maintained her weight. Hospital staff and visitors repeatedly observed that her vegetative state seemed lighter. But
she never revealed a hint of a response to anything within or
without.

I touched the silky white stockings she wore to prevent clots
and fluid from forming in the legs and squeezed her calf like I'd
squeeze my wife's. Separating her portable stereo headphones
from her ears, I heard a few bars of the *New World Symphony*. I
sat down at the foot of her bed.

Sandy wandered in. He had consulted on a dermatologic
problem on the ward. "How's she look?" he asked.

"From what I see, she's in fine shape. How are you doing?"

"I'm okay," he said with convincing happiness. "I kinda treat it like she's on vacation. I don't care how long it takes. If it's months, maybe it'll help me adjust." He ran his hand up her arm and removed the headphones. "Cynthia," he said gently, "how'd you like those shirts the kids sent over? They're doing great. I'm finally getting them organized, but you know what good kids they are."

I stood to leave him alone with her. "I like having her alive," Sandy said as he flipped a lock of hair off her brow. "Touching her, talking to her makes it easier. I don't want the world to cave in yet."

TEN

LOVELY LAURA MAY of the answering service rang to say she had a patient of one of my partners, Norm Namerow, on the line. Norm has a collection of chronic-pain patients who frequently fall apart around midnight.

"Hello, Dr. Numero?" said a young, high-spirited woman. "You're the doctor, a neurologist?" I grunted and tried not to fully awaken. "Well, something odd happened." She giggled. "You see, I have this personal-injury case going, a whiplash case, and I went to a doctor who injected a spasm in my neck with novocaine. And tonight, it really hurts. So I was talking to an attorney at a dinner party who said maybe the doctor did something wrong. I've gotta find out. What do you think?"

Now I was awake. Had she ever seen Dr. Namerow?

"Not exactly," the woman replied. He once examined her father. But she might need to see him.

"You'll have to call your own doctor or our office between nine and five," I said coldly.

"Can't you say whether . . ." I hung up. Alertness turned to anxiety, and I thought of my father.

My mother had called earlier that evening and, after telling me that Duke seemed unusually confused, handed the phone to him.

"How do you feel?" I asked. He said he had lunch with his sister. "Are you still in pain from those ribs you broke?"

"Ribs? No. I ate the usual," he answered.

"Do your ribs hurt?" I repeated.

"Hurt? Not really."

"How much walking are you able to do?"

"The restaurant wasn't far, but Mother drove. I wasn't up to it."

It seemed as if he were listening to two conversations and couldn't selectively tune in one at a time. He was picking up only key words and extrapolated meaning from them. I wondered if his tumor had further disconnected his thalamus from his language centers.

"Can you hear me? Is the line clear?" I asked.

"Yeah. Clear as a bell. Why? Are you calling from outside?"

"I'm in Los Angeles. Where do you think I am?"

"That's right. How are my little nieces?"

Gladys got back on the line. She thought he may have taken too many of his antidepressant pills, because he kept complaining about a dry mouth. Could that make him this bad, she wondered? It could. From then on, she would hand him his medications. I'd call her tomorrow.

Laura May struck again before I was able to fall asleep. An emergency-room nurse put me on hold for a long few minutes until the doctor calling reached the phone.

"Dr. Dobkin?" he asked. "Got a twenty-four-year-old male who developed tremendous testicular swelling after having sexual intercourse this evening. There's no . . ." I interrupted. Did he want a urologist or a neurologist?

"Sorry. I told the nurse . . ." Good night, I grumbled.

About 3:00 A.M., a young woman called to report that her cluster headaches had started again and she needed pain medication. She said that Dr. Alexander, one of my partners, gave her a shot of Demerol whenever an attack began. More out of reflex than interest, I asked her to describe the pain.

"It's a boring, severe cephalgia that comes out of nowhere into my right eye and cheek." In a melodramatic whisper, she added, "I could scream. My eye reddens, my right nostril gets stuffy. It lasts a half hour, then starts again in an hour or two. And the bouts come daily for a month, then stop for four months and start again. David Alexander has tried everything. He's been so kind. Could you call ahead to the E.R. so I don't have to wait?"

She certainly sounded authentic. This was a classic description of cluster, a cousin of migraine that has been treated with steroids, lithium, blood-vessel constrictors, and oxygen. No one treatment works successfully for every victim of these horribly painful binge headaches. During my residency, a patient at U.C.L.A. committed suicide when we failed to prevent a recurrence of his attacks. I agreed to phone ahead.

I spoke to an E.R. nurse who said that she knew the cluster victim. She had come to the E.R. the past three nights, demanding an injection of 150 milligrams of Demerol. A different neurologist in our group okayed it each time. But the woman always claimed to be the patient of the doctor not on call that night. And a nurse who worked part-time at a nearby hospital recalled seeing her there nightly last week.

"Sounds fishy." I yawned. "Think she's an addict?"

"That other nurse did say she heard someone caught her reaching into a drawer of disposable syringes."

"Cancel the injection. Give her aspirin and sixty milligrams of codeine, two tabs she can use overnight, and tell her she must see one of us in the morning."

It took me at least an hour to fall back asleep, and she never showed in the office that morning. My partners traded notes on how the Demerol addict duped us, and we notified the E.R. that we would not order medications for her again. They passed our suspicions to neighboring hospitals.

* * *

159

That afternoon's first follow-up appointment was Dick Gallagher. It had been about a month since I discharged him from rehabilitation. Only a residual tingling in his big toe continued as a reminder of his illness. Any anxiety about a relapse had dissipated by his third dinner at home with the family. His strength and reflexes were normal. Already, the paralysis seemed remote, like a vivid dream, he confided.

"Have you taken your wife out dancing?" I asked.

"Yeah," he laughed. "We made a deal. I'll get out on the floor if she goes rock climbing with me. Nothing dangerous. But we're gonna do more together."

"Sounds good. Everything else okay?"

He hesitated, then said, "There does seem to be a little problem with sex. Nothing comes out."

Despite attaining a normal erection, it sounded as if he was ejaculating retrograde, or backward into his bladder. I told him not to worry. The autonomic nerves probably weren't firing in coordination because of their Guillain-Barré injury. It was bound to clear soon. I agreed to let him return to work at a desk job for two weeks, and if he felt all right, to go back to installing computers.

Harvey Block looked out the window of the exam room when I entered. His bare buttocks and spindly legs suggested he meant business about his "flat."

He turned, thumbs vigorously brushing against his fingers, and said, "Dr. Dobbins, I've got to get this penis situation straightened out." I pressed my lips together. "Tried the foreplay stuff with the wife, but my back hurt too much."

"Your back?"

"Got into bed with the wife and did, you know, some things I once read about at one of those porno shops they got in Chicago when I visited there some years back. The wife, she got a little touchy. But like I says, it's too soft."

"You still couldn't have an erection?"

"Well, yeah, Doc, but no, the bed's too soft. Hurts my back unless I stay on my side. You see, we been sleeping on a sofa-bed the last fifteen or twenty years. Bought the first one on the way back from Vegas not too long after my daughter's graduation. She's a beautician, in case your wife wants to know. Anyway, the boys in the lodge used to go play craps every winter . . ."

"Maybe you should try a bed with a hard mattress."

"Wife has this idea that a sofa-bed's easier. Just fold 'er up and the room's neat. This one's a clean woman. Would you believe she flushes the toilet at home twice before setting on it after I go and three times in a bowling alley? Gotta be a doctor to afford our water bills."

"Have you been able to maintain an erection at all?"

His eyelids closed and flickered. "Not with this strawtomatic nervous condition." As he talked about trying acupuncture and DMSO, I glanced at the object of his great concern. His penis had almost disappeared into the bulge of his hanging paunch. Maybe his testosterone was low. I'd get a urologist to worry about it. "So anyway," I heard him meandering, "this Chinese fellow's got pictures of stars and they're autographed so I figure he's legit. But ten of his needle treatments didn't help none. What do you think of DMSO?"

"It's a good all-purpose industrial solvent and shows some promise as an immunosuppressant drug. I suppose it could increase blood flow to the penis, which, when you get down to it, is what allows an erection. How about if I send you off to that urologist? And you and the wife might consider some formal counseling. Might be safer than your experimentation."

"I'll tell you, Doc. You don't know what it's like to have a flat. You don't, do you?" he asked ingenuously.

"Are you still drinking, Harvey?"

"Not a drop." His tongue lashed the corners of his mouth. "Let me be honest. It ain't easy getting into bed with the wife without a few beers." He reached for his boxer shorts. "Doc, I know these facts are subject to change. But do you really think I can't drink at all?"

"Not if you want the peripheral neuropathy to improve."

Looking disappointed, he dressed. "How are the feet?" I asked.

"Feel fine." He had not wiggled his toes once. "A little burning now and then. The blue pills and those white ones with the orange stripe did the trick. Been a bit dizzy, though."

"What do you mean?"

"Well, as long as I'm active, of course, you don't feel it. Not like when I got hit on the head in the army. Boy, was that some fight. This fellow who lives in Chicago that we saw at a reunion maybe ten years ago and me was discussing just that."

"When do you feel it?" I injected quickly.

"When I'm sitting, I'm comfortable. It's something that happens when I stand up too fast."

"You get light-headed for a moment?"

"Yeah, if you wanna get technical."

I checked his blood pressure lying and standing. No drop in pressure occurred. But under the right circumstances, it might. Squatting and prolonged sitting cause blood to pool in the legs. After one stands up rapidly, the blood takes a few beats to return to the heart and get pumped against gravity to the brain. Light-headedness results until the autonomic nervous system makes its reflexive adjustments. People with autonomic failure can neither increase their heart rate nor constrict their arteries and veins to compensate for this potential pressure drop. So when they stand, their blood pressure falls sharply and does not recover. This condition, called orthostatic hypotension, robs the brain of blood and often makes its victims fall unconscious. Once they are flat on the ground and the heart no longer must pump against gravity, they regain consciousness quickly. Harvey was not yet that disabled.

"One other thing," he said, rubbing his scalp on his way out the door. "The barber says my hairs grow faster on the left side. Now isn't that the darndest thing?"

"Guess so."

"Now how can you explain that?"

"You use the left side of your brain more than the right."

"No kidding. Wait'll he and the wife hear that."

After a lengthy consultation with a retired physics professor who had suffered a TIA and wanted to know the details of every scientific paper published about an investigational drug I suggested he take, Carol Barge appeared. She sat lotus-style on my examination table with neck and head craned forward.

"How are you?" I asked. She ignored me.

Tim responded, "She's doing great. Really. You haven't had any spells since starting the anticonvulsant, have you babe?"

His wife shifted her pressed lips side to side. With the vitality of a cold metal tuning fork, she said, "The feelings are gone. No more déjà vu. No more confusion, like I don't know where I am."

"Wonderful. Let's go over a few things." Her husband nodded gratefully.

"First tell me what the EEG and CAT scan showed," she requested with a sullen look. "Am I an epileptic?"

I explained that the electroencephalogram had recorded abnormal brain waves coming from the inner surface of her right temporal lobe—spike discharges fired once every few minutes. It could build to a hot, repetitive series of discharges and cause a seizure if not suppressed by medication. The CT scan was normal, eliminating the possibility of a tumor or most any cause of epilepsy other than a birth scar. "The tests aren't as important in deciding if you have epilepsy as your symptoms. And the cure with the anticonvulsant confirms the diagnosis." She frowned, unconvinced. "There's no stigma to having seizures. Don't worry. So, did you notice any other changes?"

"Well, I don't really feel anything anymore."

"Anything?" I puzzled.

"It's nothing."

"Please, tell me what you mean." Mr. Barge crossed his legs in his chair by the window.

"Well," she said softly and pulled her knees up to her chest, "I used to get this warm feeling a few times a week over my thighs and . . . in my vagina." She stopped, as if sorry she gave this away.

"Like a sexual arousal?" I suggested.

She hesitated. "Kind of." Carol sneaked a look at her husband, who seemed to fall into a trance.

"Go on."

"Sometimes, I even used to feel hot tingling and start contracting inside, like I was real turned on."

"Do you think you lost awareness or consciousness during this?"

"I'm not sure."

"Did you feel anything else?"

"A couple of times," she added as she rotated her wedding band up and down her ring finger. "It was, I guess, a real orgasm, like nothing I've come close to with sex. I could hardly breathe, it was so intense." Her limestone cheeks and neck turned crimson.

No patient had ever described such manifest sexual hallucinations to me as part of a seizure, but it made sense. Repeated electrical discharges from neurons around either temporal lobe's limbic system can evoke free-floating fear, anxiety, vivid memories, and odd tastes and odors. The basic animal drives that stir here include those which motivate sexual activity and its consequences—reproduction. Barge's spike discharges had ignited her most sensate structures.

"Did you tell anyone about this out-of-the-blue arousal?" I asked.

"The psychiatrist in Elmira got me to admit it," she said, almost chuckling as she examined her partly chewed fingernails. "He didn't say anything, you know, about why I'd get it. It's a kind of seizure, huh?"

I imagined her shrink salivating at the Freudian dynamics. "Yes," I said, "it's one of your psychomotor seizures. Unusual, but as real as the spells in which you took off your clothes." Tim rubbed the back of his hand under his chin.

Carol, as if to make us forget what she had revealed, unveiled new complaints. She whined that the headaches persisted despite therapy and she still felt sharp jabs of pain and a crawling sensation over the back and top of her scalp. The anticonvulsant made her wobbly and drowsy. And she wouldn't take a drug indefinitely because it might cause cancer or deform her baby if she became pregnant. Then Carol accused me of exaggerating the seriousness of the epilepsy to the Department of Motor Vehicles. They had revoked her driver's license, based on my report of her seizures. Her unexpected torrent rattled Tim and me.

I met each concern. She missed most therapy sessions, so I wouldn't expect the neck spasms to improve. And her taut neck muscles squeezed the nerve branches that pass through them on their way to the scalp, which led to the jabs and tingles in her head. If she'd relax the neck muscles, the irritation would stop. The anticonvulsant drug was proven quite safe in other patients and her blood tests showed she was on the correct dose. A little drowsiness was common shortly after starting an anticonvulsant, but would wane as her brain learned to tolerate it. And if she got pregnant, we'd monitor her blood levels closely and use the smallest effective dose. If she stopped the drug, she might suffer a grand-mal seizure and cut her fetus off from its oxygen. Finally, the DMV, by law, had to be notified, as I explained at her first visit, but would reinstate her driver's license within six months of seizure control.

None of this mattered. Barge refused any persuasion, declaring she would use vitamins and acupuncture, change to a macrobiotic diet, move away from the smog, do anything. The medication was out.

She cried inconsolably, perversely, and shouted at me, "You call yourself a doctor? Think you know everything? You don't, believe me. I've been to enough of you." She hopped off the exam table, opened the door, and added bitterly, "And to tell the truth, I stopped your drug yesterday."

The husband looked like he might come to my rescue, but instead fed into this nonsense, calling after Carol as she strode down the hall. "Babe, please. Everything will be okay. We'll go home and think about it." They departed quickly, arm in arm.

I was angry. I had put up with demanding, ungrateful people since midnight. But I had also managed Carol Barge as if she was a marvelous physiological process, not a sick woman with wracked emotions and perspective. My artless neuromedicine arose from the narrow-minded assumption that I did not need to seek her confidence or mobilize her desire for a cure.

Rene walked into the exam room and said, "You're still in here? I've got Dr. Ashburn on the line. You okay?"

"Yeah, I'll get it."

"Did you want me to make another appointment for Carol?"

"We'll see."

I slumped exhaustedly into my desk chair and pressed my aching head and neck against its high back. The calls that had disturbed my sleep last night were taking their toll. It was already close to five and I had two hours of hospital rounds to make. And here was Ashburn asking me to see another patient before I left the office. "He's had a little headache and trouble concentrating the last couple of weeks," the internist said. "I've known him ten or twelve years and he's not a complainer. Blood count and cardiogram are okay. Probably just overworked, what with all the travel his company sends him on. But could you check him out? He's in my office now and has to leave for Washington tomorrow."

By the time I drank a cup of coffee, Harrison Redstone and his wife arrived. He was as tall as a college basketball forward and thin—hollowed out like someone with chronic lung disease or cancer. His thick white hair had been turned the color of weak tea by the three packs of cigarettes he smoked and coughed on each day.

"What seems to be bothering you?"

"Nothing really," he replied with a sigh. "I think I've been under too much pressure at work and it just caught up to me."

"I see." His wife cleared her throat as if she wanted to tell me more, but I was not ready for her interpretation yet. "How long has this been going on?"

"Oh, maybe a month. Been covering for someone who retired. With all the extra work, it hasn't been easy." He was vague, perhaps intentionally, about his responsibilities. He supervised the production or testing of a weapons system for the military. "I've put in my twenty years with the company. Probably ought to retire."

"Your doctor mentioned you had some headaches recently. Can you tell me about them?"

"Nothing more than tension headaches."

"Have you had them in the past?"

"No, never even knew what a headache was before a few weeks ago. I usually get diarrhea when I'm nervous. But they're the kind of pain you see on television commercials. A nagging band around the head and all. It's there all the time and more annoying in the afternoons when my load gets so that I start to think the day'll never end." I could appreciate that sentiment.

He denied any other symptoms from my menu of complaints. He had not encountered any numbness or weakness in his arms and legs, any difficulty with vision, taste, smelling, or hearing, or any dizziness, imbalance, or loss of consciousness. And he'd had no injuries or other illnesses in the past few months. He brushed aside a few lapses in memory the last week or two—some missed appointments, mixing up some figures in a report. His slumped shoulders and red eyes pointed to the kind of exhaustion and depression that impedes concentration and then memory. But there was an odd inertia in his thinking, a slowness in shifting his answers from one of my questions to the next. I asked his wife what she thought about his recent behavior.

"He's just not the same the last few days. I mean, the sweet side to his personality was always there, like a little boy's, but the aggressive side's completely gone. I don't know. It's just that, well, we've talked about retiring for over a year and all of a sudden he wants to go ahead. Something's been building up for several weeks, that's all I know." She leaned toward me and brushed against a stack of reports on my desk. "Did Dr. Ashburn tell you that he went to work without shaving yesterday and then needed a security guard to help him find his car on the company lot before coming home? I mean, this man's in charge of tens of millions of dollars and hundreds of people."

"Let me examine him. Then we'll talk," I said, as if we shared a vague suspicion that we did not want to discuss in front of her husband.

In the exam room, I tested his cognition in my routine way. He was oriented to the date, and he repeated a string of seven random numbers and correctly repeated the sequence in reverse. He recalled the words "peaches, newspapers, and Chestnut Street" ten minutes after I had asked him to remember them, although I had to repeat the words several times before he could grasp them initially. He occasionally hesitated when recalling current events and headlines from the past few years and twice gave me the same answer to a new question that he had just given to the previous one. So Redstone could store and retrieve immediate, recent, and past memories, but not as sharply as I'd expected.

He named uncommon objects, including the parts of a wrist watch, made no errors in spontaneous speech, slowly but adequately generated a list of ten animals, and followed complex directions. There was no problem in the expression or comprehension of language by his left brain.

He copied interlocking geometric figures correctly, which meant his right brain's perceptual abilities were not obviously impaired. When I coaxed him, he interpreted several proverbs with their appropriate, abstract meaning. But it was with complete indifference about whether he was doing his best that he gave me the first similarity he could think of between two items. When I asked how a mouse and a cat were alike, he said they could both be white, instead of offering that they were both animals or living things. Indeed, he plodded through all the tests with a touch of my father's apathy and inattention. It hardly seemed possible that he could make complicated decisions about military projects.

The physical exam also troubled me. When he held his arms

straight out in front of himself with palms facing up, his right arm rotated slightly inward and drooped a fraction of an inch, as if a weight in his hand made the arm tired. And the reflex at his right elbow jerked more briskly than the one on his left. These were subtle signs of a malfunction in the motor pathways that begin their journey in the left frontal lobe. His mental slowness, more a problem in initiating thought than deterioration in memory or intellect, also pointed to frontal-lobe disease, because it is here that the executive control for organizing and planning comes together. A left-frontal tumor, an insidiously growing and until-now silent malignancy, rated high on my unspoken list of possibilities.

I told Mr. and Mrs. Redstone, "I believe there's something going on in the brain, possibly some sort of mass pressing the left side. It may be serious, but we might be able to treat it. I'd like to get a CT scan immediately and put him in the hospital."

"If it's something more than stress, let's get on with it," he said. His wife wrapped her arm around his waist. My secretary told the CT technician not to go home. We had an emergency case.

A half hour later, Redstone lay on his back, his head resting in the center of the donut-shaped CT gantry. Every few minutes, the equipment whirred and another slice of brain appeared on the screen. I felt the sort of reverence I experienced as a medical student watching in teaching conferences; priestly neurologists and pathologists would ceremoniously slice formaldehyde-preserved brains like a loaf of bread, then read into the gray and white matter of each slice with their venerable wisdom.

With the same anticipation, I leaned over the radiology technician's shoulder and saw the lowest, ear-level slice first. My bird's-eye view showed the cortical gray matter at the edges of the scan, the basal ganglia and the thalamus on each side of the spinal-fluid-filled third ventricle. We progressed through the brain, moving upward slice by slice. I studied the images so hard that I grew tempted to read something into the salt-and-pepper dots, but the anatomy was normal so far. And then, three cuts from the top, something was wrong. Dark edema fluid swept across the left frontal lobe, the kind that can harbor both benign and malignant tumors. Before the next scan, Redstone moved his head. The technician readjusted him and I waited. It was going to be a metastasis from his lung.

The next oval slice revealed a thick, gray-white crescent pressing against the brain, pushing the cortical ribbon away from its usual snug fit with the skull. The mass was large enough to squeeze the left frontal lobe like a fist closing upon a hollow rubber ball. But it wasn't cancer. It was a bulging subdural blood clot, and the force with which this so-called hematoma compressed Redstone's brain could, in hours or days, cause massive increased intracranial pressure, herniation, and ultimately death. While I had only drugs to dehydrate Larry Oubre's infarcted brain once he began to herniate, in Redstone's case there was a simple surgical cure that could not fail, as long as we wasted no time.

I paged Sam Fegelman, the neurosurgeon who had removed Nellie Fisher's cerebellar tumor. I reviewed Redstone's story with him and emphasized how much deterioration the wife noted in the past one to two days. The mass must be expanding. He agreed that immediate surgery was the safest course. In the hallway of the radiology suite, Fegelman and I presented the need for an operation to the couple. They consented without hesitation, though they appeared stunned by the speed of events of the afternoon.

I asked Harrison again, as I had in the office, if he recalled striking his head in the last month. "I've been thinking about that," he said to his wife. "Remember when I was getting out of the car a few weeks ago and hit the top of my head on the doorframe? I saw stars for a moment and a headache started. Could that be something?"

That was all it took. A sharp blow over the skull tore a few tiny veins that bridge the surface of the brain and the tough dura matter, which lines the inner table of the bony crown. Several teaspoons of blood oozed until they filled a small, tight pocket, which then compressed and clotted off the ruptured bleeders. This mass stretched tiny nerve endings in the dura and produced his head pain. Perhaps only in the past week, the pocket drew in fluid and more blood and opened like a clamshell until it separated enough to bulge into and disrupt traffic in his left cerebrum.

Redstone's cognitive symptoms began as his frontal lobes lost their efficiency at sifting through the countless synaptic messages they receive every waking moment. Ordinarily, they assess all these stimuli using rules that keep us alert to anything novel. As they make important associations, perhaps like a detective who draws conclusions from suspicious clues, they fire off appropriate responses. Redstone's frontal-lobe circuits had become partially disconnected, so inertia increasingly overwhelmed thought and behavior.

"Will you help the neurosurgeon?" Mrs. Redstone asked me.

"I haven't done one of these since I was a resident, but I'll be there to cheer Dr. Fegelman on."

With surgery an hour away, while we waited for routine pre-op blood tests and the traditional head shaving, I finished my rounds. One minor problem cropped up on rehab. Larry Oubre had a low-grade temperature. His chest sounded clear, so pneumonia seemed unlikely. I sent blood and urine samples to the lab for evaluation of a possible infection and reassured Mrs. Oubre. Larry seemed more confused to her. I explained that the brain injury probably made him less able to tolerate a fever and infection.

It was already after 10:00 P.M. in Philadelphia, so I called my mother before she went to bed. Duke seemed much less confused. He had slept most of the day, but walked with his walker better than yesterday into the kitchen for dinner. He probably had been taking too much medication. But she had new concerns.

"He told me that he doesn't need a station wagon anymore," she said. "Bruce, he finally realized that he won't get better and go back to work."

"I think he's known that for a long time. He and I have discussed it at least several times. As absurd as it sounds, he didn't want you to know how bad off he believes he's gotten."

There was a long pause before she asked, "What does it mean?"

I felt myself tremble. "Before he went back to Philly, dad said he did not want to live anymore."

"Is he going to do something?"

"I don't know what he'll do or what we can do for him. Just keep trying to get him out of the house and get friends to visit. And throw out any medications that are lying around." The hospital's overhead page repeatedly announced a phone call for me. I told Gladys I'd talk to her tomorrow. The call was from Fegelman; he was ready to operate.

I entered the O.R. in surgical greens with paper booties over my shoes and mask in place. Redstone was already intubated and anesthetized. His shaven skull, like a large misshapen grapefruit, was tightly bound in milky green, sterile paper sheets. The surgeons cut a flap of scalp away from the skull. Using a hand drill, they routed out a nickel-size burr hole a few inches above Redstone's left ear. A spurt of browned blood, like old crankcase oil, shot up and splashed across the neurosurgeon's chest. He snipped off tiny pieces of bone to enlarge the hole to the size of an eye socket. Then he scooped and irrigated out fragments of clot that looked like grape jelly. I peeked in. The surface of Redstone's brain was depressed and tinged blue gray from the force exerted by the subdural. But with the pressure relieved, blood again coursed through the thin arteries and veins that crisscross the cerebrum's surface, and the tissue began to turn back to its healthy pink-tan color. The neurosurgeon sutured the flap of skin and muscle over the hole and wrapped the patient's head in a turban of white gauze.

In the recovery room a half hour later, Redstone groggily followed a few commands I gave him and moved his arms and legs. His dented brain would expand quickly. At worst, he'd lost a small patch of cortical neurons, nothing he would ever notice. I drove home feeling more like a doctor than I had all day.

PART 3

*"Which infinite calamity shall cause
To human life, and household peace
confound."*

MILTON, *Paradise Lost*

ELEVEN

WHILE REDSTONE HAD BEGUN to gain the vitality that his subdural mass had quashed, Larry Oubre's attention span began to fade and his recovery faltered. And because his face and voice continued to be unlit by emotion, it was difficult to judge from his behavior whether or not he was depressed. However, when he drew a picture of a man during therapy with only one arm and leg and said, "Men have a body, I don't anymore," I realized he had sunk emotionally as well.

I tried an antidepressant medication to increase the amount of two neurotransmitters—norepinephrine and serotonin—that tend to be in short supply in depressed people. But his alertness and motivation still sagged. He also continued to run a slight fever without an obvious cause; the toxic effects of an infection might have been compromising the already dimmed capacity of his mind.

As I shaved Friday morning, it suddenly occurred to me that Larry might have a brain abscess. With the urinary-tract infection he had over a month ago, bacteria could have entered his bloodstream and silently seeded a patch of his stroke-softened cerebral tissue. If the scavenger cells that always move in to digest this liquefied brain, like jackals descending on a battlefield strewn with millions of neuronal corpses, could not also devour the bacteria, a pocket of pus would form. As Oubre's right hemisphere shrank, with its substance dissolving into the blood or ingested by the scavengers, the collection of pus might slowly expand. Not until the abscess produced toxic wastes or grew enough to inch against normal brain would the mass of inflammation make itself known. But a scenario like this was a rare complication.

Larry slumped into the pillows that propped him up in bed. He tried to scoop a mound of scrambled eggs with his fork, but shoved them off the left edge of his plate. Then he stirred the empty dish with his fork, looking as listless and as punch-drunk as he had ten weeks ago. His left brain was no longer compensating.

"How do you feel, Larry?" I asked.

"Feel okay," he said, still staring at his fork. All week, he had denied having headaches, nausea, or being confused—the symptoms of a brain abscess. "Something funny just happened," he added. I leaned closer so I could make out the soft, flat pitch of his words. "I smelled something funny. And then I felt strange."

"What was it like?"

"The smell? Like burning hair. And a feeling like something before." He stopped. His head and eyes tilted farther to his right. His right thumb twitched a few times, as if to prime the left cortex to put into words an image it would ordinarily have captured from his right brain. "Like something that happened before, is all. Then I wasn't part of anything."

"Did you ever have that feeling before today?"

His eyes closed and he drifted away for a few moments until I squeezed his shoulder. "Last week sometime. Like the two I got a couple weeks before the stroke."

"Before your stroke? Larry, are you sure it was before?" He

nodded yes. "Larry, please open your eyes and listen. Are you certain you experienced the odor and that strange feeling *before* your hospitalization?" His sense of time had been disjointed from the beginning. But even as I tried to convince myself that he had to be mistaken, a frightening thought came to me.

"Think so," he mumbled.

It would have been most unusual to suffer a stroke so small and silent before his massive one that it would cause only temporal-lobe seizures. Yet, if the hallucinatory smell and déjà vu really antedated his stroke, whatever caused them also caused his stroke.

"I've scheduled you for a CT scan and electroencephalogram this morning," I said. "Maybe that will provide some answers. And I'm starting you on an anticonvulsant." He shrugged his right shoulder.

Rene gave me one of her smug smiles while I sipped coffee and did some paperwork at my desk that morning. "Wait until you see your next patient, Dr. Dobkin."

"I don't need any more puzzles today," I pleaded.

"Not a problem." Violet Johns walked in behind her, dressed in a red miniskirt and a lavender silk blouse unbuttoned to her braless cleavage. I recognized her as she took a seat.

Three months ago, on one of those inert days when blow-dryer hot air and opaline smog make my temples ache as if I've swallowed a massive dose of monosodium glutamate in a Chinese restaurant, I randomly picked a barbershop near the office for a haircut. An attractive woman in her late twenties greeted me with a playful smile, gently slid her hand over my arm, and seated me on her swivel chair. Her orange T-shirt declared, "For Sale." After a brief exchange about the weather and the Dodgers, she offhandedly mentioned that this was her first week on this job, but she had been styling women's hair for two years. I felt some trepidation about her skills, but her sure strokes with comb and brush massaged me into sleepy surrender.

A sharp grunt aroused me. Looking into the wall of mirrors across the room, I saw my barber, behind my back, snort and violently ram her right elbow into her ribs. An icy wave crept over my nape. She turned nonchalantly and began to trim my sideburns, her scissors' point within an inch of my eye. I tightened my thighs, ready to leap away at any false move. Then she reached for the shaving lather, hesitated a moment, whisper-grunted "shit shit," bent her head, and rammed both elbows into her ribs and spit out "damn shit." None of the other barbers cutting hair or reading a newspaper noticed her outburst. In the second it took to swing around in my chair, she again looked serene. As the possessed woman checked the sharpness of a gleaming, straight-edged razor, I hurriedly lied that my skin was too sensitive for a blade.

"Isn't that funny," she observed. "Most of the men I've done here have insisted I use an electric razor." I didn't doubt it.

I last witnessed someone like this potential Sweeney Todd during my residency. The young man, a powerful weight-lifter, kept his obscene expletives and spasms under control as long as he concentrated on a task. But the slightest inattention brought on, up to a dozen times an hour, a sudden rush of muffled profanities accentuated by sharp jerks of arm and abdominal muscles that might throw him to the ground or down a staircase. After he cracked eight ribs in a flurry of violent snaps, he threatened to kill himself if we did not cure him.

While paying the barber, I asked, with as much tone of disinterest as I could muster, given my curiosity, whether she had ever consulted a doctor about those bursts of sound and movement.

"Did I do it again?" she responded and checked the evenness of my short sideburns with a pleased, ingenuous glance. "You know, I guess I curse a little without really being upset about anything. Been doing it on occasion for years."

"You seem to make a little jerk or grunt rather often," I soft pedaled. "It might be worth seeing a neurologist. There are medications that could help you." I wrote the U.C.L.A. Neurology Clinic number on one of my office business cards and suggested that a doctor there could help if the symptoms bothered her. She could use my name as a referral.

As she read the card, I walked toward the door and pretended not to hear her say, "I'd love to see you, Bruce, if you like. My name's Violet. Do you need my number?" I got out, relieved that none of my blood had run, but uncomfortable that she misunderstood my proposal.

In my office, she provided an enticing history. Since about age ten, she would feel a need to blow off some irritating inner pressure. A gruff, throaty sound followed by a rapid head shake like a horse throwing off water, or by a quick shadowboxer's jab, relieved the tension. Her pediatrician told her family she had a psychological disorder that would clear by the time she married. I suppose he imagined that young Violet boiled with sexual impulses.

Most times the facial winces, abdominal contractions, and rapid arm flaps struck without warning. She had become expert in public at turning an unexpected sound and movement into a semipurposeful throat clearing and brush at an unseen insect or clothing lint. Her ex-fiancé told her the tics disappeared during sleep and sexual play. I gathered she rarely held onto a boyfriend more than a few months, but she never associated this with her grunts and twitches. What recently upset her were the obscenities she uttered, words totally inappropriate to her feelings.

I walked Violet to my examination room and instructed her to remove her shoes. Everything else that I needed to examine was already exposed. Rene called me back to my desk for a phone call.

I couldn't help but remember some of the people with movement disorders I've examined in the office or seen on the street. Many had a hereditary problem that caused snakelike movements of the arms and torso, or writhing, coiled postures of the arms and legs that eventually might leave them bedridden with their so-called dystonia. One unfortunate man on the rehab unit had suffered a stroke in his anterior corpus callosum, that thick wad of white nerve fibers that connects the left and right frontal lobes. When writing with his right hand, his left hand often slapped away pen and paper or attacked its mate. The therapists were most upset by the tendency for his irrepressible left hand to latch onto their breasts and genitals. When his right hand tried to pull the left one free, "lefty" tightened its grip. As a last resort, the tormented man yelled at it. The left hand let go, but sprang against his Adam's apple, much the way that Peter Sellers portrayed Dr. Strangelove. The stroke had disconnected his left and right brain, creating an alien tentacle independent of his left hemisphere's will.

I returned to the exam room to find Miss Johns stark naked. For a moment, I braced against the doorframe slightly dumbfounded by the surprise, and her beauty. "You only had to take off your shoes," I said. "Take this gown and put it on so the back is open." I quickly returned to the hall.

Once Violet Johns covered herself in a paper gown, her exam went quickly. The barber's intellect, strength, sensation, and coordination were normal. She giggled when my hammer-taps over her tendons produced normal reflex jerks. But she did not acknowledge the two times she grunted, jerked her right shoulder up, and, in nearly the same motion, reached to pat her hair with the right hand.

I explained that she probably had Tourette's syndrome, a disease affecting about one hundred thousand Americans, which until twenty-five years ago was considered either a psychiatric illness or a bad habit. When a new drug, haloperidol, reduced the unwilled sounds and movements in most victims, physicians realized that the disease might have a biochemical basis. It seems to arise from some disorder of dopamine use in the basal ganglia, which ordinarily initiates movement by translating a thought into a subconscious action. The programming of the Tourette's patient goes awry, and self-perpetuating signals are freed from the victim's will. Haloperidol probably works by blocking receptors that are overly sensitive to dopamine.

"I'll take it," she agreed, "if you think it'll make me better. When may I come back to see you?"

"Let's see how you're doing in ten days," I said.

"I can wait," she mused and swayed her head back coquettishly.

I backed out of the room and closed the door on any thoughts of infidelity. Sandy Waterford had called, so Rene got him on the phone before she brought in the next patient. He asked for a pass home that weekend for Cynthia. He knew we could not keep her in the rehabilitation center much longer. She was not improving. So he wanted to try and manage her at home. If he could not, she would have to go to a nursing home.

"How did you make out with the pass last Sunday afternoon?" I asked.

"No problem. The kids and I set her down by our pool. She always likes the outdoors. Some friends of ours came by for a drink and I tried to direct the conversation toward her. I put a drink by her side and if someone told a funny story, I made sure they repeated it to Cynthia."

"What happened?"

"She didn't really respond until we splashed water on her legs and got a startle out of her. I think it was good for her. And the kids seemed pleased. Our friends were a little uncomfortable. Don't know if I'll bring people over this weekend. This is good for her, isn't it?"

"I suppose it's good for all of you." I promised another pass. As I put down the phone, my secretary buzzed and said that a radiologist from the hospital was on another line.

"Just saw your patient's CT scan," he said.

"Oubre's? What's it show?"

"I know you were thinking about an abscess. It's a mass of some sort, all right, but real unusual. I'm not sure what's going on."

Even without seeing the scan, I could conclude only one thing. The small details of Oubre's illness that had seemed so unusual now fit together into a dreadful diagnosis. "Keep it on a view box, will you? I'll be over soon."

Larry's CT scan was hung in a quiet corner of the bustling radiology suite. The left side of his brain appeared normal, but on the right, one-third of his skull cavity was empty except for spinal fluid. The shrunken remains of his right cerebrum, an amorphous gray peninsula of tissue, jutted out like an ear from his left hemisphere. The next series of scans proved even more grotesque. An intravenous dye used to stain diseased tissue revealed an ugly, figure-eight-shaped tongue pressing against Larry's brain stem. As it had months ago, the swollen brain, now with something else in it, threatened to compress the brain stem and shut down his vital breathing and blood-pressure centers. I tried again to match these images to abscesses I'd seen before. They did not fit.

The radiologist tapped my shoulder and startled me. "Hey, Bruce. Do you want to see the myelogram you ordered on Janice McAlpine? You're not going to believe this," he said.

"I can hardly believe this." I pointed to Oubre's scan.

"Yeah. It's bad. So what's the story on this McAlpine? It said on the requisition slip that she might have multiple sclerosis, but you're looking to rule out something pressing on the spinal cord in her neck?"

I told him about Janice McAlpine as he hung up her films. She was a teacher in her late twenties who complained that when she bent her chin toward her chest, an electrical tingling sensation ran down her back and sharp pain radiated into her upper arms. We call this a Lhermitte's sign, named after the neurologist who associated the symptom with injury to the white matter at the back of the spinal cord called the posterior columns. The axons in these columns carry signals from sensors in the skin, tendons, muscles, and joints to the thalamus, which relays them to the cortex, which, in turn, interprets them as touch, pressure, and the sense of the position of a limb.

When I asked Janice some questions from the palette of symptoms that might paint a picture of a specific neurologic disease, I hit pay dirt. Six years ago, she suddenly lost vision in an eye. Although she couldn't recall which eye was affected, she did remember that it hurt when she looked sideways. Her sight gradually returned over the next two or three weeks. The symptoms were typical of an acute optic neuritis, an inflammation of the nerve used for vision.

My examination of Janice was normal except for one disturbing finding. Scraping the end of my reflex hammer along the outside of the sole of her left foot and then angling it toward the big toe caused a momentary reflex in which the toe involuntarily cocked back and neighboring toes spread apart. This was the so-called Babinski sign, unmistakable evidence of damage in the right corticospinal tract. This long pathway carries signals for voluntary movement from neurons in the motor cortex of the frontal lobe to the spinal cord's motor neurons. It crosses from the right side of the cerebrum at the level of the lower brain stem to the left side of the spinal cord. Given the Lhermitte's sign, Janice's spinal cord in the neck was the likeliest location of disease. And with the history of an optic neuritis six years ago, the cause was probably multiple sclerosis.

I had recommended that Janice get a myelogram to be sure there was no local problem in her neck—a disk pressing against the cord, a tumor, blood vessel anomaly, or a tubelike expansion within the cord called a syrinx. And at the same time, we could check her spinal fluid for evidence of MS.

Like the bulk of neurological diseases, multiple sclerosis is a clinical diagnosis, one made from the patient's symptoms and the findings of the exam. Laboratory and x-ray studies help mostly to exclude other potential diagnoses. If a myelogram showed no impingement on her cord, we would presume that Janice had a mild case of MS. The diagnosis was even more likely if her spinal fluid showed tiny concentrations of proteins called immunoglobulin G. Most patients with clear-cut MS produce this when white blood cells called lymphocytes and monocytes penetrate the white matter in brain and spinal cord. There, they inflame, damage, or devour small islands of the myelin and some of the supporting glial cells that wrap around axons like a sheath of insulation, creating gray spots or plaques of digested myelin. Viruses, toxins from the environment, even the victim's own genes may instigate the immunological stimulus that attracts these cannibals.

A CT scan of Janice's brain might reveal plaques that had caused no symptoms or neurologic signs. The newer technology of magnetic reasonance imaging seems even better at distinguishing such so-called silent plaques. MRI creates a magnetic field (strong enough to pull metal keys out of your pocket) that speeds up the hydrogen protons flying around the water molecules in the brain until they spin at about the same rate. As the spin slows, the protons transmit radio waves that are picked up on an antenna. A different sound comes from the gray and the white matter, because of differences in the amount of water present in each. A computer translates the sound into images of normal and diseased brain or spinal cord with anatomic detail almost as real as what we see when we slice into a brain at autopsy.

Victims of MS suffer unpredictable exacerbations and remissions of their symptoms which range from loss of vision, double vision, clumsiness and imbalance, and weakness or paralysis, to incontinence, impotence, loss of feeling, and the annoying sensation that an electrical current is running through their muscles. Attacks may recur years apart. About half the people who suffer repeated attacks find themselves confined to a wheelchair within ten years.

If Janice McAlpine's symptoms were from MS, then the first plaque erupted in one of her optic nerves and blinded that eye temporarily until, luckily, it healed and restored her vision. I had peered with my ophthalmoscope through her pupils and studied the visible end of each nerve. When permanently damaged, an affected nerve turns as pale and bright as a full moon, but Janice's appeared to be normal pink-orange disks.

When I was a medical student, a young woman came into the Temple University Hospital complaining that she had gone blind in one eye for a few minutes while lying in the hot sun on an Atlantic City beach. My neurology professor sent her off to take a hot bath. As his entourage of house staff and students crowded around her in the steaming bathroom, the woman went blind again in the same eye. Minutes after she had cooled down, her sight returned. The heat had caused visual signals conducted through a previously silent plaque to slow down or stop, as if all the traffic on a busy four-lane highway had to converge into a single lane. And my teacher's magic trick was exciting enough to turn me toward a career in his specialty.

A more recent and far drier way to pick up silent damage to the optic nerve is to test for a visual evoked response. The eye watches a moving checkerboard while electrodes on the scalp at the back of the patient's head record the brain waves transmitted along the optic nerve and the brain's visual paths into the occipital lobes. A delay in the speed of the waves produced suggests a block in transmission due to a plaque. Janice's evoked-response signal was slowed in her right eye.

McAlpine's second plaque presumably developed in the back of her spinal cord. Since Janice had not lost the sensory function of these white-matter columns, the plaque announced its presence, like the spark between two wires connected to a battery, when she bent her head and stretched the demyelinated fibers. A tumor or slipped disk in the neck could also deform and excite this path when she flexed her head.

The radiologist had injected dye into the spinal fluid in her low back and ran the liquid up into the patient's neck by tilting her body head-down. The flow of dye stopped at the fourth cervical vertebra only halfway up her neck. Something blocked its passage.

"The spinal cord looks a little fat on these views," the radiologist said. "Could be a tumor."

"A tumor?" I put up other views of the neck as they dropped out of the x-ray developer. "Look at this." I laughed. "It's a disc." The cushion of tissue called a cervical disc that normally is positioned between the third and fourth vertebrae had somehow slipped and worked its way against her cord. Duke's doctors originally thought something like this accounted for his numbness and awkward gait. In her case, a neurosurgeon could drill out the disk in a rather simple operation and cure her.

I told Janice McAlpine that her symptoms weren't from multiple sclerosis.

"I guess that's good," she replied. "Not that I want surgery." She rubbed her neck. "Are you sure I don't also have MS?"

She had me cornered. "We can't be certain that you won't develop symptoms of MS in the future. From ten to fifty percent of people your age with an optic neuritis like the one you had eventually get other symptoms. Not necessarily serious ones. And of course that means that fifty to ninety percent never get the disease. Let's take care of the neck. I'll send a neurosurgeon by to explain the surgery."

Mrs. Oubre stood guard by the entrance to the rehabilitation wing. She stopped tugging on the thin gold chain around her neck when she saw my reluctance to speak.

"I wanted you to tell me what the brain scan shows before you talk to Larry," she said.

I leaned my shoulder into the wall and forced myself to meet her eyes. "We're not sure what it means. There's a garland of blood vessels and brain tissue that has grown into what's left of his right hemisphere. It's not quite what an abscess might look like. And I've never seen a CT scan of brain matter look like that after a stroke." I straightened up and added, "We'd have to do a biopsy to know for sure."

"What else could it be?" I walked her down a corridor to a bank of picture windows that overlook a driveway and court-yard paved in red Spanish tiles.

"There's a chance he's had a tumor growing from his brain substance." I felt a chill run deep in my neck. Since I awakened that morning, I had clung to the increasingly remote chance that Larry's deterioration, and then his bizarre CT-scan image, might be a treatable abscess. But the scan reminded me more of a malignancy called a glioblastoma. This monster grows from astrocytes—cells that normally protect and support the neurons—gone out of control.

Ethel Oubre touched a finger to her necklace. "I don't understand. He had a stroke. You and the others told us it was just a complicated stroke."

"I'm starting to believe Larry's story about having some little seizures weeks before the warning signals of his stroke. It's possible that the astrocytes had begun multiplying in a malignant way quite some time ago. The middle cerebral artery, the major source of blood to the hemisphere, branches off the carotid artery near the inner temporal lobe. Tumor could have jutted out and grown around the artery like a clamp, until it shut off blood flow and caused a stroke. It's possible, even if it seems incredible."

"How can so much happen to one man?" She sighed. "What's going to become of him?"

"I'm sorry it came to this," I said. She sounded as desperate as my mother did when she called me last night. Duke had fallen again and cracked two ribs. His brief improvement in the rehabilitation program no longer held off the inevitable. She had to become his caretaker or find someone to stay with him at all times. Like Ethel Oubre, she would have to take control of her husband's life.

I suggested an arteriogram for Larry first. It would show where the middle cerebral artery was plugged along its course. If blood flow were cut off at a point unusual for atherosclerosis and clots, that would point to a tumor. Also, the blood vessels feeding into the mass might help differentiate tumor from abscess. The vessels in tumors sometimes fan out like cracks in a plate of glass. Abscess vessels make a thin, circular capsule around their pocket of pus. But in the end, we'd have to remove and examine a piece of the tissue in order to clearly distinguish between the two. And as careful as the neurosurgeon might be, his biopsy could cause rapid swelling, herniation, and death.

"And if it is a cancer?" she asked.

"We could radiate it, but that would probably not cure him. Maybe it is an abscess after all. For now, I'll put him on steroids again to dehydrate the swelling around the mass. That should make him more alert. Then you and the family can tell me if you want to go ahead with the arteriogram and surgery."

"But you would recommend the arteriogram and biopsy."

"If there's any chance this is a something we can treat, I'd risk surgery." She sank her chin into her chest, then threw back her head and shoulders.

"We got a locum tenens, a young internist, to cover Larry's practice. Do you think I should try to sell it while it's still worth something?"

"Even without this new problem, with just his stroke, I can't imagine him ever again taking care of patients. I guess I'd try to get some money out of what he's built up over the years."

"He'll have to know if I do it." She looked out the large window.

Across the courtyard, Sandy Waterford practiced with a therapist on lifting and transferring his wife from her wheelchair into the reclined seat of his station wagon.

Mrs. Oubre said, "I told Larry about the Waterfords. He shook his head and said, 'Isn't it terrible what can happen to someone?'" She turned to me. "Do everything you can. Even the brain surgery."

TWELVE

MRS. HENDERSON THANKED ME for fitting her husband into my Monday-morning office schedule. "Please look at Samuel with an open mind. We want another opinion. Back home, they say he'll never practice again and I can live with that. But I want at least some piece of him back. You're our last hope." She stole a glance at Dr. Henderson and reassured herself that he had not detected her deep despair. Then she measured me with intent, gentle eyes.

Samuel Henderson had opened his practice in 1950 in a small Missouri town and worked until last winter, when he simply forgot how to be a doctor. Before then, Patricia Henderson proudly pointed out, he had kept the ills of thee generations of townspeople under control with his general-practitioner's artistry.

Until the Henderson's went fishing a year ago this past summer, the physician had been in good health. "He was occasionally absentminded," she said, "but everybody puts the sugar bowl in the fridge or milk in the bread box once in a while." A few days after they reached their mountain cabin, Dr. Henderson became ill with a fever and headache and seemed mildly confused. At a nearby infirmary, a doctor suspected that a virus, perhaps the flu, caused the illness. But Mrs. Henderson, worried by his malaise and forgetfulness, ended their vacation and drove to a hospital in Kansas City where her husband had referred complicated cases for years. She handed me copies of their reports. A thorough evaluation there, including blood tests, spinal-fluid examination, and CT scan of the brain, revealed no clear cause for the illness.

He returned to work, but she said that he did not regain the enthusiasm with which he had always handled office patients and house calls. And he seemed subdued on social occasions. His patients noticed no change and lauded his kindness and diagnostic acumen as always. In the fall, the G.P. developed a slight hand tremor and shuffle in his walk. After another consultation, his physicians placed him on a medication for possible Parkinson's disease. His intellect apparently appeared normal to them.

At a Christmas party, Samuel's nurse confided to Mrs. Henderson that she had gradually begun to direct his day's activities rather closely, had to remind him about details of a patient's prior visits, and increasingly had to be available when he wanted to mull over a case with her. While the nurse had always handled phone calls about runny noses, sore throats, muscle aches, and emotional crises for patients she had known for years, she gradually found herself extending those skills to deal with more complex symptoms. Mrs. Henderson tactfully confronted the doctor with this report. He answered, "Guess I'll have to give Nurse Wessock that raise I promised."

A month later, the G.P. told his wife about a peculiar experience. He had diagnosed the acute appendicitis of the Andrews's boy. Henderson assisted, as usual, at the surgery, but the G.P. fumbled with his forceps, scalpel, and gauze sponges as if they were mismatched parts to some new mail-order gadget he wanted to connect, but had no instruction sheet. His surgical colleague grew flustered and finally said, "Nothing's working for you here. Let me finish while you wash up."

A few days later, Mrs. Henderson found the doctor putting his feet through the armholes of his undershirt, struggling helplessly in a mire of stretched white cotton.

"Samuel, what are you doing? Why are you hopping around in your underwear?"

He desperately grappled one more moment and pulled the shirt up his left thigh. Then he straightened upright as if caught in an embarrassing act. "Don't know what it is about these things, dear," he said sheepishly.

Mrs. Henderson took her husband back to Kansas City for a re-evaluation, despite his protests that he felt as well as ever. Again, most tests were normal. The CT scan showed a mild loss of brain substance, perhaps more than they might have expected for his age, but unchanged from the summer. A psychiatrist wondered about a pseudodementia—intellectual impairment from depression. When intelligence tests revealed that Henderson's I.Q. had dropped to 80, their suspicion of a progressive, untreatable dementia with irreversible loss of his memory was confirmed. They recommended retirement.

Any of the various components of memory may deteriorate in a diseased brain. The overall process of recall has been divided into short-term, or working memory, and long-term memory, the storehouse of all our knowledge. Working memory decays in minutes when it's not needed or used. It is manipulated in the sea-horse swirls of hippocampal neurons at the inner border of each temporal lobe, which are linked to the wishbone-shaped limbic path that ties in emotional drives. Working memory fails dramatically in people who suffer spells of so-called transient global amnesia, or TGA.

Another physician referred himself to me after an attack of TGA while making his Saturday-morning hospital rounds. That day, he wrote notes in the charts of the four patients listed in his appointment book, then drove home. His wife reminded him that they had plans to visit her niece that afternoon. He asked her what the time of day was. Five minutes after she answered, he repeated the question and she asked him if he were going deaf. Not three minutes later, he again asked for the time of day and where he was. She sat him down and asked if he was okay. He told her that he had to make his rounds at the hospital. She reminded him that he had made his rounds. A few minutes later he repeated his need to make rounds. This persisted for several hours, then completely cleared. The next morning, he made rounds and could not recall having seen his patients the day before or writing notes in their charts, yet everyone he talked to said they had not noticed anything unusual about his behavior then. The notes, however, said only, "Patient checked." Blood flow to both of his inner temporal lobes, especially to their hippocampal neurons, presumably had stopped for a short time, which prevented him from forming any new memories. But since his long-term memory was unaffected, he had been able, in a fashion, to carry out habitual activities.

Victims of a disease called Korsakoff's syndrome, most often malnourished alcoholics with thiamine and other B-complex vitamin deficiencies, are also unable to retain new information and usually have spotty recall of information from the past few years. In general, their attention span, ability to repeat something immediately after it is given, distant memory, language, and overall intelligence are normal, so they *can* gain access to previously acquired knowledge and use it. At autopsy, we usually find permanent damage to the inner temporal lobes and their nearby connections.

When long-term memory fails, as eventually happens in a progressive dementia, the victim loses his access to formerly acquired knowledge and has great difficulty organizing and understanding ongoing events. He increasingly cannot make associations with the concepts his mind has learned. The networks of neurons that store, interrelate, and produce facts, language, ideas, images, even sensations, become disconnected throughout the brain. What were once well-used, reliable paths erode until they no longer exist.

Alzheimer's disease is the most common cause of a progressive cerebral degeneration. This was the dementia that the Kansas City doctors diagnosed in Samuel Henderson.

In 1907, Alois Alzheimer described the disease that rhymes with "old-timer's" and accounts for the dementia of two out of three Americans, perhaps ten percent of people over sixty-five. Alzheimer autopsied the brains of his patients and found reduced numbers of cortical neurons and peculiar, shrunken nerve cells with tangled, clumped branches surrounding a pink plaque of proteins called amyloid. The amyloid may be nothing more than a waste product of dying cells, but some researchers wonder if it might be a protein from a virus that might cause the disease. Surprisingly, the area around hippocampal neurons reveals few tangles and plaques. But the cells that funnel what we see, hear, smell, and touch into the hippocampus are devastated. The neurons that transmit memory information from hippocampal cells to the rest of the brain also shrink and die. So while the hippocampal centers are prepared to receive and send out what's newly learned, the progressive destruction by whatever causes Alzheimer's disease disconnects them from the rest of the cortex and they become an abandoned island.

In 1980, neurochemists discovered that brains autopsied from deceased Alzheimer's victims contain less of the neurotransmitter acetylcholine than normal brains. The neurons that manufacture and release acetylcholine reside in the underside of the brain in the nucleus basalis and extend their axons to the hippocampus. In young people, about a half-million cells are at work in the nucleus basalis, by age sixty-five only two hundred thousand remain, and in demented people fewer than one hundred thousand survive. It may be that as these producers of acetylcholine fall below a critical number, memory impairment begins. When the neurons they stimulate die off and fall below another critical number, especially around the hippocampus and its limbic connections, then memory, emotions, and attention slowly grind to a halt as well.

At first glance, the acetylcholine deficiency seems analagous to the dopamine deficiency in Parkinson's disease. But, so far, attempts at jacking up brain acetylcholine have not improved memory, concentration, and behavior in any practical way. As sometimes happens in Parkinson's, the neurons activated by the substance we provide artificially can become too shriveled to respond. And there seem to be deficiencies of other neuro-transmitters and their receptors that confound our attempts to treat the disease.

Dr. Henderson had a modest hand tremor and slightly stiff walk. He also demonstrated what we call motor impersistence; when I asked him to close his eyes and keep them that way, he could keep them shut for only a second. And the G.P. showed more than casual forgetfulness. Aftere several tries, he gave me the correct month and year, but missed the day of the week. I had to repeat a phone number three times before he could re-cite it correctly. He spelled the words "cat" and "hand" forward and in reverse, but could not concentrate enough to spell "world" backward. When, after three minutes, I asked him to recall the random words "peaches, newspapers, and Chestnut Street," the doctor perseverated with "cat." The last president he could name was "that bad fellow." He spent over a minute copying a triangle drawn within a circle. "Don't do that very often," he excused himself. When I asked him to cal-culate the number of nickels in $1.20, he answered "a dollar and twenty." Nor could he interpret any abstract meaning from a proverb or common saying. When I asked him to ex-plain what people mean by the expression, "Someone has a heavy heart," he said, "Guess somebody had a coronary." He looked at me with the sort of congenial, polite smile you see in people who miss the humor in a joke and do not want to appear left out.

The Kansas City records and my history and exam left me with a diagnosis of the incurable dementia of Alzheimer's dis-ease. I strongly suspected that it had been smoldering for some time before their vacation, but that his wife and nurse had overlooked how often they had compensated for his lapses in memory and judgment until his errors had become gross in the last year.

"It just can't be," Mrs. Henderson cried. "We've taken care of so many people with that at the nursing home." I handed her a tissue. "It's just that sometimes he seems so much better. We can take a walk and he knows his way around, asks about different patients, even tells me about something he read or saw on TV."

"That's about right," the doctor injected. His wife smiled kindly at him. Dutiful, lovingly rational, gently manipulative, she would not easily lose Henderson to his ungovernable mind.

"People with Alzheimer's can seem better, especially in a familiar routine. Sometimes they remember recent events that have a special meaning, an emotional impact." She looked unconvinced. I imagined that the doctor had never given up on a patient, even if a comforting touch was his only treatment. Now, Mrs. Henderson believed doctors had written off her befuddled physician. "What's he like at his worst?" I asked.

"I don't know," she murmured. "Yesterday at our nephew's he thought I was fixing his lunch. It was eight in the evening. He couldn't lay out his clothes. And he slipped into thinking we were back home."

Dr. Henderson nodded his head wistfully: "Sometimes we can't be sure of things. I'm not much of a dresser anyway." His voice still bore a compassionate rhythm, the kind of charm and strength that puts patients at ease.

"Do you remember eating at your nephew's last night?" I asked.

"Not really," he said pensively. He pulled a suspender with his index finger.

The wife frowned. "I know you're gonna think I'm going off the deep end, but what do you think about chelation therapy? I heard from someone on the plane coming into Los Angeles about a clinic here."

"Aluminum has been found in a high concentration in some

Alzheimer's victims at autopsy, and chelation could remove some of it, but, so far, where the treatment has been tried in a reasonably scientific way, it hasn't improved anyone. And these chemicals can cause serious side effects."

"I figured as much. Wanted to be sure." She paused and watched Dr. Henderson's hands folded in his lap. "It's just that sometimes he really changes, sometimes it's not just that he's slower, he doesn't seem to be able to think or move *at all*."

An idea popped up again that had crossed my mind but had seemed too far-fetched. "Can you give me an example?"

"Yes!" she blurted. "Yesterday, he started for the kitchen table barely able to lift his feet, then froze in his tracks. He hardly responded to us. We asked if he was tired and he nodded, so we brought over a chair and sat him down. At home when it happens, I lay him down in bed, and in an hour or less he'll get up on his own without a complaint. I've checked his blood pressure and I've given him orange juice in case it's a sugar problem when it happens, but he comes back in his own time."

"You mean he'll stand there as if his feet are stuck to the ground?"

"Yes, that's what it's like. Very strange. Never saw that in our senile patients."

"You told me he has normal control of his bladder," I said, not yet willing to uncork a burgeoning possibility. "At times like this, when he seems worse, has he ever wet himself?"

"I don't think so."

"I've wet myself," Dr. Henderson admitted. He concentrated his gaze on her, as if to warn her not to cover up for him. "I dribble on myself without realizing it. Been meaning to have the prostate checked out."

"I just thought those were little accidents from not pulling down your pants soon enough," she said, not sure whether to trust his recollection.

But I wanted to. It raised the possibility of a different diagnosis, something treatable. I picked my words carefully, testing the logic of this diagnosis as I spoke.

"We might be dealing," I said directly to the physician, "with a block in the absorption of your cerebrospinal fluid. The butterfly-shaped ventricles centered deep in the brain constantly produce CSF. Normally, the CSF exits the ventricles and slowly flows over the surface of the brain, and a balance is struck between the amount made and the amount absorbed into the veins on top of the brain. If it is not absorbed quickly enough, the trapped pool in the ventricles slowly expands. Eventually, it compresses and injures nerve fibers alongside the butterfly wings. Memory, gait, and bladder control suffer most, because nerves from the frontal lobes involved in these functions pass by the ventricles. My guess is that when there's a sudden wave of high pressure in the fluid, your feet stick to the ground and your thinking and bladder control get acutely worse."

Through much of the sixteenth century, European scientists thought the ventricles were more important than the brain. At the time Leonardo da Vinci poured the first wax cast of the ventricles from an ox's brain, the chambers of the butterfly cavities were assigned the function of common sense, imagination, and memory. In reality, they serve as sewage drains that soak up waste products from neuronal metabolism. The CSF produced in them also cushions the brain from bruises against the hard skull.

"Haven't heard that one," Henderson mulled. "Medicine's getting away from me. This is informative, isn't it, Mother?" His wife gripped the arms of her chair, ready to leap.

"Can we do anything?" she asked, almost afraid to know.

"If we can prove the pool is stagnant," I answered, enjoying the intellectual and emotional fit of my proposed diagnosis, "a neurosurgeon can pass a thin plastic tube, a shunt, through a hole drilled in the skull to the wings and then drain them slowly."

Mrs. Henderson asked, "What are the chances it'll work?"

"We have several tests that can help with the diagnosis, but the best test is the surgical treatment. If he improves, he has what we call normal-pressure hydrocephalus. If he remains un-

changed, then he doesn't. The surgery could cause life-threat-
ening complications, though, so it shouldn't be taken lightly."

I suggested we start with an x-ray study called a cisterno-
gram. If the results were typical of NPH, then I would urge
taking the risk of surgery for what I guessed was a fifty percent
chance of success in halting Henderson's dementia. If the test
results were not typical, then we'd have to make a crapshooter's
decision. The Hendersons agreed.

I repeated the doctor's CT scan that afternoon to compare
the size of his ventricles to what they were eight months ago on
the Kansas City scan. If CSF pounded the walls of the ventricles, I'd expect the butterfly wings to have enlarged. But their
size and shape were unchanged. That did not disprove a diagnosis of NPH, but I felt discouraged.

At noon, Fegelman, the neurosurgeon, grimaced dolefully
when he saw me in the doctors' dining room. I walked over and
asked quietly, "What did you find on Oubre?"

"No problem with the surgery," he said. "The brain was
slack when we opened and the surface yellow and firm. I don't
expect too much post-op swelling. We made several passes with
a biopsy needle into what looked like a soft gray tumor. The
first report from the pathologist is a glioblastoma."

"Jeez."

"Sorry. Maybe it would have been better if he died in the
beginning. I did MacAlpine's cervical disk after Oubre. She's
doing fine. Can't win them all. You know, I didn't tell Ethel
Oubre. Thought you might want to wait until the permanent
biopsy slides are ready."

"I'll go check what they have. His wife's got to decide what
to do for him. By the way. I admitted a fellow who might have
normal-pressure hydrocephalus. I'll let you know on Thurs-
day."

"That's such a hard diagnosis to prove. You think you've got
one?"

"For his wife's sake, I hope so."

In the pathology lab, the microscopic tissue I examined from

Larry's biopsy was so distorted that it didn't even seem to come from a brain. The pink background stain was punctuated with macabre dark-blue blobs that still seemed alive. These oval and pear-shaped, giant-size cells were inhabited by ugly nuclei, frozen in the act of malignant multiplication. In places, deep columns of these cancerous cells spread out from a central blood vessel as they invaded neighboring tissue.

Larry lay in the surgical intensive care unit with his scalp puffed up over the three-inch wedge of skull removed for the biopsy, too groggy to talk. Mrs. Oubre handled the news with the delicate restraint of someone expected to take illness in stride.

"Is there any hope with the radiation therapy?" she asked.

"It might prolong his life by a matter of months."

"Can it be done as an outpatient?"

"I suppose so. It won't be easy to take care of him. But we could help train an attendant."

"Can I decide in a few days?"

"Of course." I suspected she had already studied her options and knew her decision.

In the late afternoon, I reviewed the first set of Samuel Henderson's films. The radiologist had injected a radioactive dye into Henderson's spinal fluid. Instead of following a normal drainage path up the spinal column and over the convex surface of the G.P.'s cerebral hemispheres, the radioactivity had begun to diffuse into his ventricles. A speckled outline of a butterfly with opened wings started to take shape. I told the Hendersons the test might be positive, but we'd have to watch for another forty-eight hours to see if the dye stagnated or cleared.

Mrs. Henderson bowed her chin against clasped hands and sighed, "Two days."

The doctor lightly admonished, "These things do take time."

Two days later, some radioactivity still sparkled in the central wings and some capped the brain's surface. So absorption took place, though slowly—a possible, but not classic picture for NPH. I had seen surgical shunting fail in demented patients with identical films. One of them died from a bacterial infection that inflamed the pool a month after surgery. I did not want to jeopardize what remained of Dr. Henderson's health.

I discussed the test results as Mrs. Henderson pushed her husband in a wheelchair across the gray macadam parking lot toward a gangly hedge of oleanders. The air smelled of fertilizer that had been spread over seeds of winter rye grass. The G.P. toyed with a shirt button at his navel, as if it were the head of a stethoscope.

"Do you want to talk it over with the docs back home?" I finished. She massaged her husband's shoulders from behind.

"We'll go ahead with surgery and trust the Lord," she said.

"I'd be glad to help if it's surgery," the doctor added.

Fegelman operated on Friday. Orderlies wheeled Henderson into the surgical ICU as I arrived. His arms and legs were moving, so at least the shunt, pushed several inches through the cortical surface into his right ventricle, had not caused paralysis. But he did not recognize me. He spoke incoherently about delivering a baby on a golf course. As I walked over to check Larry Oubre, I hoped I had not harmed Mrs. Henderson's husband.

Larry sat in bed with his head bandaged in a white gauze cap. The swelling over his forehead and eyes that made him look like a boxer after a knockout had nearly disappeared. I asked how he felt and he whispered, "Good. What did the biopsy show? Any bugs?" He had been too drowsy the past three days to understand what it revealed.

"They haven't grown any bacteria yet. There was a lot of necrotic tissue from the stroke. But we'll keep checking the cultures."

"No pus, huh?"

His mind was more alert than his hoarse, emotionless voice led me to believe. I wanted to wait until Monday to talk about this, when his wife had a clearer plan. But he reached for my hand and looked for an answer in my eyes. "We saw tumor cells," I said. For a moment, I felt as if I were again telling Duke that he had a brain tumor. "A glioblastoma, I'm afraid."

Larry lowered his head and whispered something I couldn't make out. Tears wet his lashes. I squeezed his hand and once again repressed my impotence and grief. "I'll do everything possible," I said. But he knew the prognosis.

THIRTEEN

FEGELMAN WAS WAITING FOR ME in the doctors' lot. It was a crisp, late October day; maple leaves had turned red orange and newly sprouted rye grass greened the center of the track used by the cardiac-rehabilitation patients.

"I saw Sam Henderson in the office yesterday," the neurosurgeon said. "The shunt's draining fine."

"It's been, what, two weeks since you put it in? How did he look?"

"I think he's better. So does his family. Didn't really test him, though. They're supposed to see you today. You started radiating Larry Oubre?"

"His wife wanted it." I hadn't encouraged or discouraged her. She was not yet ready to give up all hope for a cure. We might buy Larry a few extra months of life, and if he were spared the side effects my father had suffered, some of those months might be good ones. "She decided against adding chemotherapy," I said. "The problem now is that he's getting nowhere with rehab. If anything, he's regressed again."

The steroid we'd given him kept the edema from encroaching on his brain stem. But even if we destroyed 99.9 percent of the glioblastoma cells with radiation therapy, the wildly growing survivors would double every few days until they gutted Larry's left cerebral hemisphere and choked off his brain stem.

"Got anything else cooking for me?" Fegelman asked.

"You kidding? You'll have to invest in an avocado farm to shelter yourself from the tax man." I smiled. "I'll call upon your golden fingers if I need them."

Fegelman loved to open a spine or skull and fix things up. Doing a spinal tap and injecting or manipulating a muscle spasm is as close as I ever get to probing the body like a surgeon. I regret not doing more hands-on things for patients. Sometimes, I even become physically restless, like a spectator watching a sports contest he knows he could be playing. As much as I enjoyed the ritualistic hand scrub outside the operating theater's doors and the pomp of the surgeon's decisive calls for "scalpel, hemostat, retractors, sutures, tie, scissors, and cut" during my surgery rotations in medical school, I could not get past the notion that surgeons seemed prouder of their unambiguous actions and meticulous cutting techniques than of the logic of their treatments. Neurology, on the other hand, is a game of words and observations. I take some comfort from another notion, that "the men of action are, after all, only the unconscious instruments of the men of thought," as Heinrich Heine put it.

From the doorway to Larry's rehab room, I watched Mrs. Oubre shuffle containers on his breakfast tray. She daintily poured a measured amount of milk and sugar into his oatmeal and scraped up a half teaspoon of cereal. With her left hand under his chin, the thumb lightly against his neck, she offered the spoon to his lips, then in synchrony with him, opened and closed her mouth each time he cleaned off the oatmeal.

When she spotted me, Mrs. Oubre said, "Dr. Dobkin's here, honey. Shall I tell him what we've been discussing?" Larry started to reach out his hand, but it got stuck under his tray table. "We'd like to be discharged this coming weekend."

I was happy to send Larry home at last. Mrs. Oubre would hire a nurse's aide to live in their home, and we'd provide a commode, wheelchair, and hospital bed, and arrange outpatient radiation. "So how's my good man doing?" she asked.

"His blood chemistries look fine. No evidence of lung or bladder infection. Everything is stable."

"That's good. Did you hear that, Larry? No serious problems."

"Going home, huh?" he mumbled.

"I'm so glad we've gotten through all this," she added and walked me to the door. "My son and I want to thank you for getting Larry along this far."

She never blamed me for not making the tumor diagnosis sooner. "The real work is ahead of you," I said.

"You do what you can." She pressed her lips together and raised her eyebrows with a sigh.

"Call me anytime. I'd like to check Larry when he's done with the radiation. We can try to taper him off the steroids by then, before they cause side effects. But let me know immediately if he gets a fever or has trouble swallowing."

Harvey Block stood in the lobby of the office building. "Hi, Doc Dobbins."

"Hi. Coming up to the office?"

"No, going to check out my new leg with the man upstairs."

"Leg?"

"You know, that prostitute he's got blowing up my flat. The penology doctor." Harvey's fingers made no movements. "It's really something. Don't go down right. Maybe the plumbing needs work. Gives the wife the wrong idea. Thinks I'm some kinda sex maniac." People edged past us. "She's never liked mechanical things anyway. No understanding of 'em. Did I tell you that she thinks you shouldn't drink the tap water in the bathroom when the toilet's flushing, in case there's a backup? And she's always flushing . . ."

"Mr. Block . . ."

"I'm telling you, I knew she was some kinda hard woman.

Saw that in her mother. And then there was that class reunion a coupla years ago we went to. Started this whole thing. In front of these old friends, and some of them looked awfully old, I could hardly believe they was my age, she tells 'em I don't get it up for her. She's the one never wants to start until everything's sanitized."

It wasn't an ideal spot to discuss Harvey's penile prosthesis and manage his circumlocutions. I walked to the stairwell instead of to the elevator, so he wouldn't follow me, and called back, "Phone my secretary if you think we can help any further with your neuropathy."

"Oh, that's no problem, Doc. You finished off that one, but . . ." I hurried up the steps.

Rene handed me a chart and said Violet Johns was already in an examination room. The lady barber wore another revealing pink silk blouse and a red leather skirt hemmed at midthigh. Sitting on the exam table, she wriggled her trunk and flared her nostrils at a near-frenzied pace and described intense anxiety and restlessness. Her medication, haloperidol, sometimes causes this for a few weeks, but a second drug often reverses the symptoms until they fade naturally.

"Hey, I can't live like this. And that stuff hasn't even stopped my cussing."

"I know it's hard to believe this, the way you feel," I responded, "but you'll probably come to tolerate it, and eventually we'll be able to try the higher dose we'll need to control the sounds and jerks. Or, I can switch you to a drug that might have fewer side effects."

"You're trying to help and I appreciate it, really, but this stuff sucks. I mean, it's worse than my problem, which doesn't bother me, I guess, as much as it bugs other people. I'll try the drug again if I absolutely need it."

"That's fine. The drug isn't a cure. It only reduces symptoms. Contact me whenever you want. I can send your records to another physician if you want to try another tack."

"Thanks," she said with a glow. "Here, I brought you something." She lifted six vials with pastel-colored lids from her pink, wet-look bag. "They're organic body oils that get rubbed into your skin; fruit flavors."

"Sounds wonderful," I said. "Bet Barbara, my wife, will be interested."

She laughed politely, and with a sudden snap of her head backward and simultaneous forward flinch of the right shoulder, walked out the door.

Dick Gallagher called. "I worked at a desk and then tried to get back on a truck doing installations," he said. "I'm exhausted by midafternoon. This isn't some kind of relapse, is it?"

He said he wasn't having any trouble lifting things or climbing ladders, and that he didn't have any numbness in his hands and feet. The problem with retrograde ejaculation persisted. It sounded to me that he just lacked the stamina he needed for his job. The recovered axons in his peripheral nerves had to fire their muscle fibers more often than usual to compensate for still-damaged ones, and that cost Dick energy. I told him not to worry and sent him back to his desk for another few weeks and recommended that he build up his endurance by working out on a stationary bicycle for twenty to thirty minutes a day.

Dr. and Mrs. Henderson were in the corridor telling my secretary about a planned excursion to Hawaii. Henderson walked slowly, but without the stiff heaviness of two weeks ago. They greeted me effusively and giggled like teenage lovers about sightseeing the past few days. Then Dr. Henderson said, "Hope you don't mind if I say so, but your wallpaper hanger hung your bamboo trees upside down." It was true. Only a few people had ever noticed that the angle of the leaves defied gravity. He was better, but I was still skeptical.

So I gave him my usual tests and found that his memory, figure copying, reasoning, and the rich content of his speech reflected the cognition of a rather bright man. Only arithmetic and proverb interpretation stumped him a bit. Mrs. Henderson, no longer needed as his advocate, slipped quietly into the background. I was astounded by his turnaround. I asked the

G.P. if he could describe what the past few months had been like.

Dr. Henderson deliberated a moment, then paced the room. "I didn't realize how bad off I was. A little slow, yes, but not going crackers. Everything I did seemed an effort, like my mind and body were tired."

"Do you recall our conversations about testing you for normal-pressure hydrocephalus and doing the shunt?"

"Well, I knew decisions had to be made, but I couldn't quite think them through. I felt kind of bewildered; not afraid of making a mistake, not troubled, just somehow bewildered. The wife knew better."

It seemed that at least some new information had been getting into his working memory, but he could not find a way to retrieve or manipulate it. Perhaps what he did register wove itself into his memory like the vague thoughts we experience in the twilight as we awaken or are about to fall asleep.

"Tell me again what caused all this," Henderson asked.

"I have to guess it was a virus," I suggested. "Probably a mild inflammation scarred down the tissues responsible for absorbing spinal fluid and ruined the delicate balance between production and removal."

"And the shunt runs the excess off," he finished. "Mother sure picked a good man for a second opinion."

"You chose a good wife," I said. "She did the real work." I promised to forward his records to Kansas City.

As the couple passed by Rene, the G.P. turned back to me, grinned, and said, "No offense, but you forgot to have me repeat, 'peaches, newspapers, and Chestnut Street.'"

FOURTEEN

S HE'S IN PERFECT CONDITION. Not a blemish on her skin."
Sandy winked at his kids and placed a hand on each of
their heads. They had waited in the hospital lobby while
he made Sunday rounds. "We're gonna pick Cynthia up now
from the nursing home."

"Mommy looks around," said the youngest daughter. "Not
exactly at you, but she moves her eyes and lets us talk to her."

Sandy hugged the girls against his hips. "It was great when I
found I could carry her down to the pool myself and stretch her
out on a chaise. She's a little stiff, but really light. I read to her
and we hold her hand. Cyn always loved the outdoors. Maybe
she feels the sun and hears the wind chimes we bought in La
Paz before the accident. Who knows?" His daughters skipped
over to nearby swivel chairs and spun themselves.

"The girls like to visit the home and do Cynthia's hair in
braids or do her nails. They push her wheelchair outside and
talk over things. We used to go almost every weekend, but
things come up and we visit about twice a month. What's neat

about it is that both kids told me they'd rather have her like this than not have her at all."

"Sandy, do they think she's going to get better?" I asked below the girls' singsong humming. It had been eight months since her discharge from the rehabilitation program.

"They don't exactly think she'll be normal again. But they believe that she appreciates what they say and do for her."

"How are *you* doing?"

"Okay. I've got a housekeeper the kids like. But it's pretty lonely sometimes. Cyn and I shared everything. I'm still not real comfortable treating myself to dinner out and sitting alone in a restaurant. Last week, I talked it over with the girls and we decided it would be okay for me to date. Maybe this summer when they go off to camp."

I've always expected people to consider survival in a persistent vegetative state to be worse than death. But for most families I've met, it's different. As long as the loved one suffers no pain or indignity, they'll hang on to hope. Everyone's bought a lottery ticket that has no better than a one-in-several-million chance to win; why not take a gamble with brain disease? Ethel Oubre might have felt the same way.

A week after Thanksgiving, Larry had completed his course of brain radiation without mishap. His eyes were drawn as if by magnets to his right and he was unable to move his lips or mouth to speak, but he reached out and grasped my hand. I decreased his dose of steroids. In late January, he became drowsy and vomited for days. His tumor had spread to his left brain and his intracranial pressure had increased dangerously. We could boost his steroids or let the disease take its course. Mrs. Oubre said that she was not yet ready to let go, so I tripled his dosage and he became alert enough to be fed and tell her if he was about to have a bowel movement.

A month before Easter, Mrs. Oubre returned to my office with her husband. Larry was very thin. It had been taking her an hour to feed him a dozen teaspoonfuls of pureed food. He said nothing and recognized no one. His right arm and leg had grown weak and stiff with bent contractures like those that had set in months ago in his left limbs.

Mrs. Oubre said, "He doesn't seem to know us anymore. Didn't think he'd last this long."

"You've done an incredible job."

"I guess it can't go on much longer. We'll keep trying."

I spoke with her on the phone a week later. Larry had begun to choke when she fed him.

"There isn't any future here, is there?" she asked.

"He's past the point where he appreciates what you do."

"I'd hate to see him with a tube in his stomach or in the hospital again. What would you do?"

"I'd stop the steroid."

"I'm not very brave. Maybe I should lower his dose. I think I can do that."

"That's fine. Call me if there's a change."

Rene handed me a phone message two days later from Ethel Oubre. It read, "Larry died in his sleep. Thanks for putting up with me." I stuffed the note in my shirt pocket. At night, I left it on my dresser with other messages from patients and their families for whom I had no answers.

A request for Carol Barge's medical records came from an upstate–New York neurologist. I scribbled, "Handle her with care," at the top of my typed history and physical. Maybe she would finally get the help she needed for her epilepsy.

Raul Compos's wife wrote in her Easter card, "May you be as blessed as we are blessed by your care of Raul. If only he could get back to what he used to be." I was at the limits of my craft with Raul. Fueled by the dopamine and steadied with a walker, he was able to walk room-to-room in his home, but not outdoors. Arthritis limited him as much as the stroke and Parkinson's.

Harvey Block was refurbished with his second penile prosthesis and had stopped drinking. He no longer needed my direction, but I found that I missed our encounters.

Dick Gallagher was expecting his third child and got promoted to supervisor. The study of plasmapheresis as a treatment for the Guillain-Barré syndrome concluded that the procedure tends to give the most severely weakened patients their strength back faster and more fully, but the effect of the bloodletting is less than dramatic.

Samuel Henderson's wife wrote to me from their home. Samuel had tried to return to work, but in his absence two young doctors from a nearby town had taken over most of the patients in his practice and rounds at the local nursing home. The few loyal patients he saw part-time eyed him suspiciously. Everybody knows your business in a small town, Mrs. Henderson pointed out, and they understood that his judgment depended on a thin tube burrowed under his scalp. And Mrs. Henderson still worried too. Almost daily, she pressed her finger against the shunt's bulb behind his ear to check for the firmness that indicated cerebrospinal fluid flowed out from his ventricles. After he made some clumsy moves in a game of chess, the doctor called me and asked if I was sure he did not suffer with Alzheimer's. His own doubts and the scrutiny of others led him to retire on New Year's Day.

Duke had refused to spend the winter with us in Los Angeles, where good weather would have allowed him more freedom. I visited him in Philly in April. He was at his best. He glided his walker correctly and spent most of the day out of bed. He even took me out for a lunch of steak sandwiches, rice pudding, and steaming hot coffee. We talked about Barbara and the twins, about my brother Craig's adventures on his climb of Mount McKinley, and the job my sister took managing the paper-goods store in which my mother worked part-time. We even planned that he'd visit us in California. But the doctor saw the changes a son would not acknowledge. Duke's right leg dragged more now than last summer, and he had to drink his coffee with both hands. And his mind still wandered. The night before, Gladys had asked me, "You didn't expect him to live this long, did you?" I had not. He might go on for years in a slow progression of disability, with clouded thinking and stumbling gait.

On the third day of my visit, he fell down in his bedroom. The chronic pain in his neck and back got worse, and except for trips to the bathroom and to the kitchen for dinner, he stayed in bed. His thoughts kneaded the past—friends who died in World War II, business decisions that had not worked out, former employees and acquaintances whose obituaries he read, conflicts in family affairs that no one but he could recall. He ate candy bars and tuna fish and drank only decaffeinated coffee. I treated him with drugs, ice packs, and massage, but the pain reawakened his depression.

Before I left, Gladys brought out the old family albums. "He was such a proud, handsome man," she said. He did appear gallant in his corporal's uniform. She handed me the letter he wrote in May 1943 from a base in North Africa. It ended: "All in all, from the time our 107th Medical Detachment hit Algiers, we did our share and lived through enough gruesome nightmares to last me the rest of my life. These are only comments—nothing exaggerated—just showing how the boys took things as a matter of course. What is in store for us now, I don't know."

At the end of July, a year after Dick Gallagher, Larry Oubre, and Cynthia Waterford joined him at Daniel Freeman for what Duke had believed would be his last chance to get well, Gladys came home from work to find him sitting on the floor, propped up by the side of his bed, dead from a heart attack.

Before Duke's death, I mostly avoided the pain and sadness that surrounds neurologic diseases by becoming caught up in an abstract cerebral landscape. I marveled at what my patient's diseases taught me about the brain and apportioned the burdens of disease to the naturalness of bad health and death. That seemed to be the only sane way I could stare repeatedly into the face of tragedy. But Larry, Cynthia, and Duke fused my detachment and compassion into a more natural alloy, and now I always feel Duke's cold hand in mine when I try to comfort a patient or family.

After the funeral, the twins met me at the door to my mother's home. Both girls squinted for a moment and tightened their jaws, exactly the way my father and I do under stress. Then, with all their twenty-two-month-old intensity, they chorused, "Daddy go away. Goes to work. Comes back now."

I squeezed them and whispered, "Yes, he goes to work and he comes home."

Acknowledgments

My thanks to John A. Drimmer, Barbara Grossman at Crown, and Liz Darhansoff for unflagging encouragement.